The Joy of Baking

The Joy of Baking

by Barbara Grunes

ideals

Publisher	Patricia Pingry
Cookbook Editor	Teri Mitchell
Copy Editor	Peggy Schaefer
Art Director	David Lenz
Pasteup Artist	Kris Ray
Production Manager	Jan Johnson
Consultant	Mildred Brand

Foreword

Inside these pages is a new, comprehensive collection of recipes designed to fulfill the growing interest in baking. The skills needed to become successful in the baker's art are taught in *The Joy of Baking*.

All the information needed to become an expert baker is available through the detailed explanations of basic techniques, step-by-step photo sequences illustrating the preparation of six basic types of batter or dough, and full-color photographs of the finished products.

There are informative and helpful charts, hints, and tips, plus a glossary of terms. There is also a special section illustrating how to decorate cakes easily and artfully.

In "Cakes, Flans, and Small Sweets," the basic technique for making butter cakes is taught, along with how to turn this batter into a variety of tortes, cookies, and flans.

"Tortes, Gateaux, and Cake Rolls" teaches the technique for making sponge-type cakes, jelly rolls, and other specialty cakes.

"Tarts, Pies, and Cookies" teaches the technique used to make kneaded dough into pies, cakes, strudels, cookies, or tarts.

"Breads, Rolls, and Pastries" shows how yeast can be used to create delicious pastries and high-rise breads for breakfast or dessert.

The "Gift and Specialty Baking" chapter expands on the use of yeast in creating flaky, filled pastries. There is also a section on how to use sour cream to bake delicious, moist pastries, cakes, and tarts.

In "Puff Pastry and French Pastries," learn how to use frozen puff pastry to make cream puffs and eclairs, or create delicate, flaky pastries from scratch. There is also a section on deep frying some of the batters and dough to make crullers, doughnuts, and other sweet treats.

A helpful cross-referenced index at the end of the book aids in quickly locating a favorite recipe or selecting a new one.

The Joy of Baking will provide even the novice baker with a sense of security in the kitchen. Enjoy each chapter to the fullest, while savoring each delectable morsel fresh from the oven.

Table of Contents

Basic Baking Equipment

Cookie presses help to form large quantities of cookies with only one filling of the press. The cookies are pressed directly onto the baking sheet. Molding plates can be changed even when the cookie press is filled with dough. Some cookie presses are also available with decorator tips and can be used like a pastry bag.

Measuring cups come in two types: dry and liquid. To measure dry ingredients, fill measuring cup to overflowing and level off with a knife. Liquid measuring cups are see-through so the liquid can be poured to the correct level.

Pastry bags with various tips are used to decorate cakes with frostings and cream fillings and to pipe out cookies and assorted dough.

Pastry wheels can be used for cutting or making decorative designs on kneaded dough.

Rolling pins can be made of wood, plastic, or marble. The best types are heavy with ball-bearing roller action. They are indispensable for evenly rolling out dough. Rolling pins with tapered ends rather than handles are excellent for rolling out bread dough.

Scrapers or rubber spatulas aid in removing bits of pastry batter and dough from the mixing bowl and in spreading dough evenly in baking pans.

Sifters are used to loosen flour and other dry ingredients in order to remove lumps and incorporate air. Sifting should be done before measuring, unless otherwise directed.

Wire racks are especially useful for cooling just-baked cakes, cookies, and pastries.

Wire whisks come in many sizes and are used most often to beat eggs or cream.

The best pans for baking cakes, breads, and other pastries are those that have satin-finish bottoms and shiny sides. These types of pans allow even baking and browning.

For pies, a pan or plate made of a dull metal or a glass or ceramic pan will aid in heat absorption and in browning the crust.

Baking or cookie sheets are used for an assortment of pastries and cookies.

Cake pans are usually round, square, or rectangular.

Jelly-roll pans are long shallow pans about 1-inch deep. They can be used for cookies and pastries, also.

Loaf pans are rectangular in shape and are used with breads or some cakes.

Springform pans have removable sides that can be taken off completely.

Tart or flan pans usually have fluted edges. Some have removable bottoms. The center of flan pans is usually raised.

Tube or bundt pans have a center tube to help the cake rise through more even heat distribution. Many tube pans have removable bottoms.

Baking Ingredients

Baking powder is a chemical made predominantly from sodium bicarbonate. It is sold as double-acting baking powder and should be stored in a cool, dry place, away from strong-smelling spices.

Baking soda is a chemical made of sodium bicarbonate that becomes a leavening agent when mixed with acidic ingredients such as molasses or buttermilk. Baking soda disintegrates into the air when allowed to stand and should be kept in a well-sealed container in a dry place.

Spritz Cookies

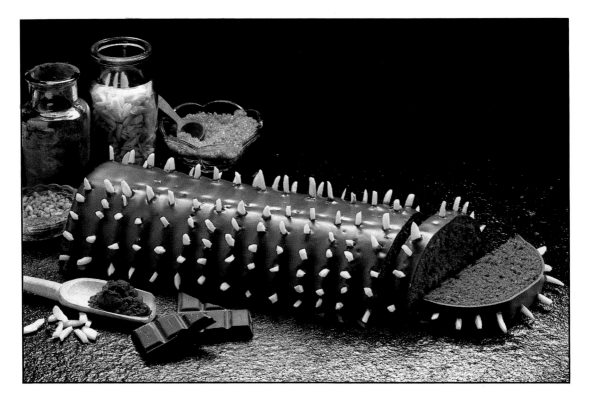

Chocolate Almond Cake

Brown sugar is a moister sugar made with molasses. It ranges from light to dark brown, with the darker colors having a stronger flavor. When measuring brown sugar, it should always be firmly packed into the cup.

Butter or margarine adds a rich, distinctive flavor to baked goods. The recipes in this book use unsalted butter. If you have only salted butter on hand, omit the salt called for in the recipe.

Confectioners' sugar, also called powdered sugar, is the equivalent of the European icing sugar. It tends to lump and should be sifted if needed before measuring. It is often sifted lightly over baked goods for a decorative touch.

Crème Fraîche is a nutty-flavored cream used in Europe somewhat similar to sour cream. It is now available in some parts of the United States. To make your own, combine 1 cup whipping cream and 1 teaspoon cultured buttermilk in a saucepan. Heat to 85°.

Remove from heat and let stand at room temperature (65° to 85°) until thickened. Stir, then chill until ready to use.

Eggs should always be fresh when used in baking. Break each egg into a cup before adding to other ingredients. The eggs will smell rotten if they are bad. Do not use eggs with red streaks in them. If the recipe calls for egg whites, be sure there is no yolk mixed in with them or the egg whites will not beat to a fluffy consistency. The eggs called for in the recipes in this book are large eggs.

Flour is available in many types: all-purpose, whole wheat, rye, specially milled cake flour, and more. Flour should be kept in a dry place. All the recipes in this book use all-purpose or cake flour unless otherwise noted. Use enriched flour to add vitamins and nutrients to baked goods.

Granulated sugar is used to sweeten

baked goods. It can be used for meringues, sweet dough, cakes, and more. The sugar called for throughout this book is the familiar white granulated sugar unless otherwise noted.

Milk and cream are used frequently as liquids in baking recipes. Half-and-half, evaporated milk, sweetened condensed milk, sour cream, and whipping cream are all very important ingredients used in baking.

Whipping cream or heavy cream should be at least a day old to whip to the highest volume. For best results, have bowl, beaters, and cream well-chilled before beginning.

Sugar comes in many forms and is used for many types of baked goods.

Yeast is a biological rising agent that comes in 2 forms: fresh yeast cubes that must be kept refrigerated for best results, and also ¼-ounce packages of active dry yeast. The organisms in yeast produce carbon dioxide and alcohol from carbohydrates, resulting in the rising action.

The subtle use of **spices, flavorings,** and **extracts** can set baked goods and pastries apart from ordinary, everyday desserts.

Allspice is the berry of the Jamaican pimento tree. The taste is a combination of cinnamon, cloves, and nutmeg. It is used ground in desserts and sauces.

Anise is a spice from the fruit of the anise plant and has a strong, sweet, spicy flavor often used in cookies. The aroma evaporates quickly, so it should be bought in small quantities just prior to use.

Caraway seed is an aromatic spice from the fruit of the caraway plant. The seed can be bought whole, ground, or powdered. It is a hearty spice used in pastries, bread, and rolls.

Cardamom is the dried seedlike pod of the cardamom plant. It is available whole or ground. It has a hot, spicy flavor and is often used instead of cinnamon or cloves.

Cloves are the dried aromatic flowers of an evergreen tree of the myrtle family. They are used whole or ground. Cloves have a strong, scented, hot flavor.

Ginger, spice from the dried roots of the ginger plant, is often used in baked goods. It can be bought whole or

Almond Bread

ground, and can be preserved in syrup. Ginger has a strong, spicy, somewhat hot flavor and should be used only in small quantities.

Mace is the spice obtained from the inner shellcase of the nutmeg. It can be bought whole or ground. Mace has a more delicate flavor than nutmeg.

Nutmeg is the spice from the seed of the nutmeg plant. Grated nutmeg is used for baking. It is best when freshly grated.

Poppy seed are the seed of the poppy plant. They are used ground as a filling or whole as a dough ingredient. Whole

seed are also used to sprinkle on rolls and bread.

There are many varieties of **flavorings and extracts**. The familiar vanilla, almond, and lemon extracts are used frequently in baking to impart a special flavor to cakes and pastries.

There are also specialized flavorings such as chocolate, raspberry, and lime. Flavored liqueurs are also used sparingly to add a touch of emphasis to certain baked goods.

Almonds are nuts that can be bought whole or shelled, toasted or blanched, with or without skins, ground, chopped, grated, or slivered. They may also be ground to make marzipan or almond paste.

Candied orange or lemon peel is usually available cubed or halved. It is used for decorating and in preparing dough and fruit cakes.

Coconut is usually used in baking in the grated or flaked form. Fresh coconut should be stored only for a limited time because its high fat content will cause it to spoil. It is available canned or frozen. If using flaked coconut, use 1⅓ cups flaked to substitute for 1 cup freshly grated.

Currants are available fresh or dried. The dried currants should be soaked for 10 to 15 minutes in warm water and then drained before being used.

Pecans are nuts from the pecan tree. They are used in pies, pastries, and cakes. They are sold in the shell and shelled, halved and chopped.

Pistachios are small oval nuts from the pistachio tree. They are usually sold already shelled. Finely chopped pistachios are used in dough while coarsely chopped or halved pistachios are used for decoration.

Raisins are small air-dried berries from

Tea Cookies

various types of sweet grapes. They are used in pies, cakes, cookies, and other confections. They come in light and dark varieties.

Walnuts are nuts from the walnut tree. They are sold in the shell and shelled, halved and chopped. They are used in cakes, icings, and pastries.

Solving Common Baking Problems

Ingredients

Egg whites will not whip. Egg whites will not whip up stiffly if there is any trace of grease in the bowl. Be sure your bowl is clean. Egg whites also will not whip if there is any yolk mixed in with the whites. If egg whites still will not beat up into the proper volume, try adding ⅛ teaspoon of cream of tartar for each egg white used. If beating eggs in a copper bowl, do not add cream of tartar because the acid in the cream of tartar will cause the whites to turn green.

Yeast does not bubble or foam. Yeast needs warmth to work properly. Compressed yeast works best when the temperature is about 80°. Packaged active dry yeast works best around 110°. Be sure your liquid is at the proper temperature to activate the yeast. Active dry yeast is helped by the addition of sugar. If mixture does not foam after 10 minutes, the yeast is probably old and no longer active.

Dough Preparation

Dough breaks apart when kneading. Dough may break apart when kneading due to a lack of shortening or liquid. If this occurs, press a small hollow in the center of the dough and add a little milk; work the milk in using a fork to spread it throughout the dough. The dough should then hold together and it can be kneaded.

Dough is too soft to be kneaded. Sometimes dough will be too soft to knead because of the high proportion of butter in the dough. If this happens, cover the dough with plastic wrap and chill in the refrigerator until dough is firm enough to work with.

Dough is too sticky to be kneaded. This problem can occur if too much liquid was added or if too little flour was used. Knead in more flour, a little at a time, until dough is of proper kneading consistency.

Dough cannot be rolled out after kneading. This problem is most often caused by the margarine that is used. If you are using margarine instead of butter, be sure to use solid margarine and not the "spreadable" or "soft whipped" margarine.

Cakes

Cake is burned. The oven temperature may have been too hot. Check oven temperature with an oven thermometer and adjust accordingly. The oven may also be heating unevenly. Place cake pan in center of oven to assure even circulation of air flow.

Cake browns unevenly. This can be caused by improper oven temperature and circulation of the heat in the oven. This can also be caused by the ingredients not having been well blended. Be sure to combine the ingredients thoroughly before placing in cake pan.

Cake runs over sides of pan during baking. This can be caused by using the wrong pan size or by using too much sugar, baking powder, or baking soda.

Cake falls apart when being removed from pan. This can be caused by too low an oven temperature or incorrect baking time. Be sure to follow recipe directions and test cake for doneness before removing from oven. This prob-lem can also occur when too much butter, sugar, baking powder, or baking soda is used. Be sure to cool cake in pan for 5 to 10 minutes before attempting to remove it from the pan.

Cake sticks to pan or crust falls off. This can occur if the pan is not properly greased or lined. Also, too much sugar may have been used or the cake may have been in the pan for too long before removal.

Cake is higher on one side. This can occur if the oven rack is uneven or if the oven does not heat and circulate heat properly. The batter could have been spread unevenly in the pan or the cake pan may be warped.

Cake did not rise. This can be caused by using an incorrect amount of baking powder or baking soda. It also may happen if the pan is too large for the amount of batter, or if the oven temperature is incorrect.

Cake fell. This problem can be caused by using too much sugar, butter, or liquid. It can also be caused by not using enough flour. This also happens when the cake was not baked for the proper amount of time, or if the oven was not hot enough.

Cake crust is soggy. The cake was

probably not baked for the proper amount of time or the oven temperature may have been too low. This can also occur if the cake is left to cool in the pan for too long before inverting onto a wire rack.

Crust is not browned properly. The oven temperature may not have been hot enough. Not enough sugar, butter, baking soda, or baking powder was used. Using too large a pan can also cause this problem.

Top of cake is cracked or too rounded. This can be caused by using too much flour or too little liquid. Overmixing the batter can also cause cracking. This is also caused by not spreading the batter evenly into the pan or by having the oven temperature too hot.

Cake is soggy and heavy on the bottom. This can be caused by improperly mixed ingredients, too much liquid, too little baking soda or baking powder, or improperly beaten eggs. The bottom of

Light Glaze

Chocolate Glaze

some ovens may not heat as well as the top part and this can also cause the problem.

The whole cake is heavy. This is often caused by overmixing. Also, using too much butter, liquid, or flour, or too little sugar, baking powder, or baking soda may lead to this problem. The baking temperature may have been too high.

Cake is tough and chewy. This problem is caused by using too much flour or too little butter or sugar. The batter may also have been overmixed, or perhaps the oven was too hot or the cake was baked too long.

Cake is sticky. Using too much sugar often causes this problem. It can also be caused by baking for too long or not cooling the cake properly.

Cake is coarsely grained. This can occur when the butter or sugar is not creamed until well blended. It can also occur if too much baking powder or

baking soda is used, or if the oven is not hot enough.

Cake has air bubbles. This happens when the batter has been overmixed when adding the flour. Stir in flour only until well blended.

Cake is dry and crumbles when cut. This often occurs if too much flour, baking powder, or baking soda is used, or if too little sugar, butter, or liquid is used. The cake may have been overbaked at the wrong temperature.

Fruit or nuts sink to the bottom of the cake. This problem can be solved by heating dried fruits in warm water, and then draining before adding to the batter. Fruit and nuts can also be tossed briefly with flour (or cocoa, if making a chocolate cake) before adding to the batter.

Pastry

Pastry shrinks when baked. Pie or flan pastry should not be stretched to fit

Fruit-Topped Sponge Cakes

the pan. It should fit loosely over the sides of the pan and then be molded into shape.

Pastry crumbles. This can be caused by overmixing the dough or handling and rolling it out too much. It can also be caused by not adding enough butter or by adding too much liquid.

Pastry forms blisters. This can be caused by stretching the pastry too much or, in the case of a pie crust, not pricking the crust enough before baking.

Pastry does not brown. The oven temperature was too low.

Pastry bottom is soggy. The oven temperature was too low. This can also be caused by using too much filling or a filling which is too runny. When making a filled pie, you may wish to prebake the bottom crust for a few minutes.

Pastry is too thick, too doughy, or too soft. Not enough butter or liquid was used or the oven temperature was too low. This can also happen if the pastry is rolled out too thickly.

Pastries cannot be removed from pan. Sticking can be prevented by following the instructions for greasing the pan or by using a non-stick pan. Pastries should be removed from the pan when they come out of the oven and placed on a wire rack. If pastries still stick, put the tray back in the warm oven for a few minutes.

Deep-Fat Frying

Frying in deep fat is the process of submerging dough in hot oil and frying until it is cooked and golden brown. You can use a deep cast-iron skillet or saucepan with high sides or an electric fryer. Fill the skillet with 3 to 4 inches of oil, or if using an electric fryer, follow manufacturer's directions.

Heat the oil to the temperature called for in the recipe. Test the oil by using a frying thermometer. If you do not have a thermometer, you can test the heat of the oil with a cube of bread and a timer.

Cut a 1-inch square bread cube and drop it into the hot oil. Time how long it takes the bread to turn golden brown, then determine the temperature of the oil by using the following guide:

340° - 355°F (175° - 177°C) in 65 seconds
356° - 365°F (180° - 185°C) in 60 seconds
366° - 375°F (186° - 190°C) in 50 seconds
376° - 385°F (191° - 195°C) in 40 seconds
386° - 395°F (196° - 200°C) in 20 seconds

After frying a batch of food, let the temperature come back up to the required heat before adding any more food. Retest temperature to be sure. Skim out any loose bits of dough or batter before frying any more batches, or the bits will burn and affect the flavor of the food.

Apple Flan

Baking Temperatures and Conversion Guide

For cakes and pastries to bake properly, the oven temperature must be regulated. You can purchase a small oven thermometer and place it in the oven to check the temperature. If your oven heats above the temperature shown on the thermometer, adjust the temperature given in the recipe downward accordingly. Adjust recipe temperature upward if your oven underheats.

For example, if the oven thermometer registers 375° when you have preheated to 350°, then adjust your oven to 325°.

Oven Temperatures

	Fahrenheit
Very Slow oven	250° - 275°
Slow oven	300° - 325°
Moderate oven	350° - 375°
Hot oven	400° - 425°
Very hot oven	450° - 475°
Extremely hot oven	500° - 525°
Broil	550°

To convert Fahrenheit to Centigrade, take the Fahrenheit reading, subtract 32 from it, multiply the result by 5, and divide that result by 9.

To convert Centigrade to Fahrenheit, multiply the Centigrade reading by 9, divide the result by 5, and add 32.

Testing Baked Goods for Doneness

Before removing baked goods from the oven, it is best to check to make sure that they are thoroughly done.

Certain varieties of baked goods have special tests to check for doneness.

Cakes should be baked without opening the oven door for the minimum amount of baking time given in the recipe before they are tested. For the majority of cakes, insert a wooden skewer near the center of the cake all the way through to the bottom and pull it back out. If the skewer comes out clean, the cake is done. If the cake is a flat jelly-roll style cake or if it is a sponge-type cake, lightly press on the top of the cake near the center with your fingertips. The indentations should spring back immediately if the cake is done. If the cake is not done, bake for 5 to 10 more minutes and retest the cake. The cake will also begin to pull away from the sides of the pan when it is done.

Yeast breads are tested by removing the bread from the loaf pan or baking sheet and tapping the bottom of the loaf with your fingertips. The bread will sound hollow when it is done. The bread will also pull away from the sides of the pan when it is done. If the bread does not sound hollow when tapped, return the loaf to the pan and bake 5 to 10 minutes longer, then retest.

Fruit or nut breads can be tested by using the wooden skewer. Place skewer in the center of the bread and pull out.

If the skewer is clean, the bread should be done. If not, return the bread to the oven and bake for 5 minutes. Bread may be removed from the pan and baked directly on the oven rack for 5 minutes if you wish to have a browner crust.

Cookies should be baked for the minimum amount of time directed in the recipe before testing. However, keep a careful watch that they do not get overly brown. Use flat cookie sheets with no rim to aid in even browning. If using 2 cookie sheets at a time, the baking time may need to be lengthened.

Pastries should be baked for the minimum amount of time given in the recipe. Pastries are usually baked until golden brown. If you feel the pastries are browning too quickly, cover them with a sheet of foil.

Equivalency Chart

Ingredient	Amount	Equivalent to
Apples	1 large	1 cup sliced or chopped
Bananas	3 medium	1½ cups mashed
Berries	1 pint	2 cups sliced
Butter	1 stick (¼ pound)	½ cup
	4 sticks (1 pound)	2 cups
Chocolate, bittersweet	1 square	1 ounce
Chocolate chips	6 ounce package	1 cup
Cocoa powder	8 ounces	1 cup
Coconut, shredded or flaked	3½ ounce package	1⅓ cups
Cream		
sour cream	8 ounces (½ pint)	1 cup
whipping cream	½ pint	1 cup
whipped cream	½ pint	2 to 2½ cups
Eggs		
whole	5 large, 6 medium, 7 small	1 cup
whites only	8 to 10 whites	1 cup
yolks only	10 to 12 yolks	1 cup
Flour		
all-purpose	1 pound	4 cups
cake	1 pound	4¾ cups
Gelatin, unflavored	1 ounce	¼ cup
	1 envelope	1 tablespoon
Lemon	1 medium	3 tablespoons juice
Lemon zest (grated peel)	1 medium	1 tablespoon
Milk, evaporated	6 ounce can	⅔ cup
sweetened condensed	14 ounce can	1¼ cups
Nuts, shelled		
almonds, ground	1 pound	2⅔ cups
almonds, slivered	1 pound	5⅔ cups
peanuts	1 pound	3 cups
pecans, halved	1 pound	4 cups
pecans, chopped	1 pound	3½ to 4 cups

walnuts, halved	1 pound	3½ cups
walnuts, chopped	1 pound	3½ cups
Oranges	1 medium	¾ cup diced
Orange juice	1 medium	6 to 8 tablespoons
Orange zest (grated peel)	1 medium	3 to 4 tablespoons
Peaches	4 medium	2 cups sliced
Raisins	1 pound	3 cups
Sugar		
brown (firmly packed)	1 pound	2¼ cups
granulated	1 pound	2 cups
confectioners'	1 pound	4 to 4½ cups
Yeast	1 cake	4 teaspoons
	1 package (¼ ounce)	1 scant tablespoon

Emergency Ingredient Substitutions

Ingredient/Amount	Substitution
Baking powder, 1 teaspoon	¼ teaspoon baking soda plus ½ teaspoon cream of tartar
Cornstarch, 1 tablespoon	2 tablespoons all-purpose flour
Chocolate, 1 square unsweetened	3 tablespoons cocoa plus 1 tablespoon butter
Cream, half-and-half, 1 cup	1½ tablespoons butter plus ⅞ cup milk
Cream, sour, 1 cup	⅓ cup butter plus ¾ cup buttermilk or yogurt
Cream, whipping, 1 cup	⅓ cup butter plus ¾ cup milk
Flour, 1 tablespoon	1½ teaspoons arrowroot
Flour, 2 tablespoons	1 tablespoon cornstarch
Flour, 1 cup cake flour	1 cup less 2 tablespoons all-purpose flour
Ginger, ½ teaspoon fresh grated	¼ teaspoon ground ginger
Lemon zest, 1 teaspoon	½ teaspoon lemon extract
Milk, 1 cup	⅓ cup powdered milk mixed with 1 cup water or ½ cup evaporated milk plus ½ cup water
Orange zest, 1 tablespoon	½ teaspoon orange extract
Yeast, 1 tablespoon (1 package)	1 compressed yeast cake

Baking at High Altitudes

Cakes and pastries rise quicker at high altitudes than they do at sea level. Above 3,000 feet some adjustments are needed to ensure proper baking. Cakes tend to stick to the pan more at high altitudes so grease and flour the pans a little more than usual. Because the high altitudes cause batter and dough to rise faster, the amounts of baking powder and sugar are reduced while the liquids are increased. Pastry is not so affected by the elevation, but you may wish to add a little more liquid, because it tends to evaporate more rapidly at high altitudes. Use the following chart as a basic guideline.

High Altitude Adjustments

Adjustment Needed	3,000 feet	5,000 feet	7,000 feet
Reduce each teaspoon of baking powder	⅛ teaspoon	⅛ to ¼ teaspoon	¼ teaspoon
Reduce each cup of sugar	1 tablespoon	1 to 2 tablespoons	1 to 3 tablespoons
Increase each cup of liquid	2 tablespoons	2 to 4 tablespoons	3 to 4 tablespoons

Storage of Cakes and Pastries

Cakes baked in porcelain molds. Remove cakes from the oven and set aside for 10 minutes before turning out onto wire racks. (Fruit flans, however, should be turned out onto wire racks immediately after baking.) Once cooled, wrap tightly in foil and store.

Cakes baked in metal pans. Remove cakes from pan while still warm. Cut cake if required and cool on wire racks. Leaving cakes in pans to cool causes moisture to collect and can affect the flavor and texture.

Small pastries. As soon as pastries are baked, remove from the pan and cool on wire racks. To keep pastries crisp, store in containers with tight-fitting lids. Soft pastries can be exposed to air until they are firm, and then stored in containers with loose-fitting lids. A piece of bread, stored with the pastries, will keep them soft. Various pastries can be layered in the same container but divide the layers with foil or waxed paper. These pastries can also be frozen.

Cookies. Be careful not to overbake cookies. When removed from the pan, they should still feel slightly soft. Macaroons will dry out while cooling on wire racks. To retain crispness, store in containers with tight-fitting lids. To keep them soft, place a piece of bread in the container.

Fruit and nut cakes and loaves. Cool thoroughly on wire racks and wrap in foil. They will stay fresh for up to 4 weeks when stored in a cool, dry place. Storing fruit cakes is especially beneficial because it allows the spices to permeate the whole cake. These cakes may also be frozen.

Freezing Cakes and Pastries

Cakes elaborately decorated with whipped cream or other toppings are best preserved if the cake is frozen first, then packed into a box or container so that the decorations will not be damaged.

If possible, pack small pastries in serving portions so you can thaw out only the amount needed at one time. These pastries, once thawed, cannot be successfully refrozen and thawed again.

Most baked goods can be successfully frozen for up to 6 months; however, they are most flavorful during the first 3 months of storage.

All cakes and pastries can be thawed in the refrigerator, left out on the counter until they are room temperature, or heated in a very slow oven.

If thawing at room temperature, it will probably take from 3 to 4 hours for a cake, less time for individual pastries. If using the oven, it will take from 5 to 20 minutes depending on the size of the baked goods.

Tortes, cakes, and gateaux with fruit or cream fillings should be thawed at room temperature, and they may take longer to thaw than plain cakes.

To make serving easier, cut cake while still partially frozen.

Type of Cake or Pastry	Suitability for Freezing	Remarks
Cakes made with butter	Good	Do not freeze cakes with jelly fillings or toppings.
Cakes made without butter	Good	Freeze decorated cakes before packaging.
Cakes made with kneaded dough	Good	Freeze without icing or fruit toppings.
Sour cream cakes and pastries	Good	Do not ice before freezing. Pastries can be rebaked lightly and then iced.
French pastries	Good	Freeze the pastries before baking, if desired. Thaw, then bake and ice.
Puff pastry	Good	Freeze without glaze. Thaw, bake lightly, and glaze.
Yeast cakes and pastries	Good	May be thawed in oven.
Deep-fried pastries	Good	Freeze before glazing or icing. Thaw in oven, and then glaze, ice, or dust with sugar.
Pastries with Meringue Toppings or Fillings	Poor	Not suitable for freezing.

Metric Measure Conversion Chart

Recipe Calls For	Symbol	Multiply By	To Find	Symbol
teaspoons	tsp.	5	milliliters	ml
tablespoons	tbsp.	15	milliliters	ml
fluid ounces	fl. oz.	30	milliliters	ml
cups	c.	0.24	liters	l
pints	pt.	0.47	liters	l
quarts	qt.	0.95	liters	l
ounces	oz.	28	grams	g
pounds	lb.	0.45	kilograms	kg

Glossary of Baking Terms

Almond paste: Blanched ground almonds flavored with sugar, orange juice, and rose water.

Bake: To cook a food in an oven or oven-type appliance.

Batter: A mixture of somewhat thin consistency, made from flour, liquid, and other ingredients.

Beat: To make a mixture smooth through the quick movement of a spoon, whisk, hand beater, or electric mixer.

Blend: To thoroughly combine two or more ingredients by using a stirring motion.

Bombe: A dessert made of cake and filling which is placed in a mold and set aside or chilled until firm.

Brush with: The process of using a pastry brush to coat foods lightly with a liquid or other spreadable mixture.

Butter: A substance made of cream and milk fat; also, the process of greasing a dish to aid in removal of baked goods.

Caramelize: The process of heating sugar over low heat until it melts and turns golden brown.

Chill: To place food in the refrigerator or in a bowl of ice or ice water until cold.

Coat: To dip or dust food with another substance until covered.

Cool:	To set food aside until it comes to room temperature; or, to chill briefly in the refrigerator.
Cream:	The fatty portion of milk; also, the process of making a mixture smooth and creamy by beating with a spoon or mixer.
Cut in:	To combine butter and flour by using a mixer, pastry blender, or two knives, until the mixture becomes crumbs of the desired size.
Deep fry:	To cook food in deep, hot fat.
Dot:	To place bits of butter or margarine over pastry.
Flan:	Sponge-type cakes which are baked in pans with raised centers so that when inverted, there is a depression in the cake that may be filled with glazed fruit, pastry creams, or a variety of fillings.
Flour:	A product made from wheat which is used in baking; also, to coat a pan or food lightly with flour.
Fold in:	To gently blend two or more ingredients together using a circular in and up motion, bringing the mixture up from the bottom of the bowl and over the surface.
Gateau:	A rich dessert made of layers of cake or pastry and fillings.
Glaze:	To brush a mixture on foods to give a shiny appearance.
Grease:	To lightly cover a dish or pan with butter, margarine, or oil to aid in easy removal of baked goods.
Invert:	To turn a pan upside down; this is usually done when placing cake or pastry on a wire rack to cool.
Knead:	The process of pressing, folding, and turning dough to thoroughly combine ingredients.
Marbling:	The process of slowly swirling a knife through batter to cut a darker mixture into a lighter one, or vice versa, creating a marbled effect.

Marzipan:	Almond paste blended with confectioners' sugar, flavorings, and egg whites.
Meringue:	A combination of stiffly beaten egg whites and sugar. The meringue can be cooked hard to form shells, or cooked soft to top desserts.
Patty shell:	A pastry shell, made from puff pastry, used to hold various fillings; they can be bought frozen and ready to use.
Pit:	To remove the seed from a fruit.
Poach:	To cook in a simmering liquid.
Preheat:	To heat the oven to required temperature before beginning to bake food.
Punch down:	To deflate risen yeast dough by pushing it down with your fist.
Purée:	To sieve food or blend it in a blender or food processor until thick and smooth.
Scald:	To heat to a temperature just below boiling; tiny bubbles will just begin to form at the edge of pan.
Sift:	To put flour or other dry ingredients through a sieve or sifter to incorporate air and remove any lumps.
Torte:	A dessert made with cake, meringue, or filling and usually layered and covered with a rich, sweet, topping.
Whip:	To beat a mixture such as cream quickly by using a mixer, whisk, or hand beater in order to incorporate air into a mixture.
Yeast:	Micro-organisms that act as leavening agents to cause baked goods to rise. The recipes in this book call for active dry yeast.
Zest:	The colored peel or rind of citrus fruit. Used grated or slivered.

Cakes, Flans, and Small Sweets

Cakes, Flans, and Small Sweets

There are two basic kinds of cake-type batter or dough. There are those made with butter and those made without butter—the sponge cakes. The batters in this chapter use butter to create a variety of baked goods, such as flans, cookies, loaf cakes, buns, and tortes.

Important Preparations

1 Combine the dry ingredients on a sheet of waxed paper.

2 Stir together the ingredients called for in the recipe, such as flour, baking powder or soda, cornstarch, or cocoa.

3 Place the dry ingredients in a sifter.

4 Sift to remove any lumps. Sifting also helps to add air to the mixture, resulting in a lighter cake.

1 Grease the cake pan with butter or margarine or shortening.

2 Add a light dusting of flour to the pan, if desired, to assure easy removal.

3 Do not attempt to flour the sides of the pan.

4 Do not use oil as it tends to gather in the corners and make the cake soggy.

1 Loaf pans may be lined with waxed paper after being greased.

2 Place the pan over the waxed paper.

3 Trace the bottom of the pan and then the sides onto the waxed paper.

4 Cut out tracings and place in pans.

The Individual Steps

1 Have butter at room temperature before beginning.

2 Cream the butter in a large bowl until fluffy.

3 Beat until light in color and texture is smooth.

1 Sprinkle sugar over butter.

2 Add sugar a little at a time to make mixing easier.

3 When all sugar has been added, blend in the vanilla.

1 Add any additional spices or flavorings called for in the recipe. If the recipe calls for such things as lemon zest, flavored liqueurs, or other flavorings, add them now.

2 Stir until well blended.

1 Break each egg into a cup before adding to the dough.

2 Add eggs, 1 at a time.

3 Beat well after each addition.

4 Beat for approximately 30 seconds to be sure they are well blended.

5 Some recipes will call for eggs to be separated. Follow the recipe directions as to when to add yolks or whites.

1 Sprinkle dry ingredients over dough a little at time.

2 Gently blend in dry ingredients until mixture is no longer dry.

3 Blend for 2 minutes.

4 Add milk or water as called for in the recipe.

5 Blend until dough is smooth.

1 Do not overbeat.

2 When lifted, dough will hang slightly from a spoon before dropping.

3 Dough should be moderately stiff, but flexible when well blended.

4 Overbeating will cause the cake to be thick and heavy.

1 Stir fruit or nuts into dough last.

2 Stir only enough to blend fruit evenly throughout the dough.

3 If using dried fruit, first soak for 10 to 15 minutes in warm water and drain well.

1 Gently spread dough into pan.

2 Use a scraper or rubber spatula to spread the dough evenly.

Baking

Bake all dough according to recipe instructions. Before removing cake from the oven, test for doneness by inserting a wooden skewer in the center of the cake. When it comes out clean, the cake should be done. Remove cake from the oven and cool in pan for 5 to 10 minutes. Invert onto a wire rack.

Frankfurt Ring

(Illustrated on pp. 30-31)

¼ cup butter *or* margarine at
  room temperature
¾ cup sugar
1 teaspoon vanilla
3 eggs
2 cups flour
4 tablespoons cornstarch
2 teaspoons baking powder
  Buttercream
  Rock Almond Topping
8 candied cherries

Preheat oven to 375°. Grease a 9-inch ring mold.

Cream butter in large bowl until fluffy. Sprinkle sugar over butter; mix well. Blend in vanilla. Add eggs, 1 at a time, beating well after each addition. Sift flour, cornstarch, and baking powder together. Sprinkle flour mixture over batter; blend well.

Turn batter into prepared ring mold. Bake for 25 to 35 minutes or until a wooden skewer inserted in center comes out clean. Prepare Buttercream and Rock Almond Topping while cake is baking.

Cool cake in pan for 5 minutes. Loosen edges of cake and invert onto wire rack. Set aside to cool. Cut cake into 3 layers with a serrated knife. Frost bottom layer with Buttercream. Repeat with remaining layers, placing each atop the previous layer. Frost top and sides of cake, reserving ½ cup of Buttercream for garnish. Sprinkle cake with Rock Almond Topping. Pipe 8 mounds of Buttercream around edge of cake; place a candied cherry on each mound.

Note: The cake is best when prepared the day before it is to be served.

Makes 8 to 10 servings

Buttercream

1⅛ cups butter at room
   temperature
 4 to 5 cups confectioners'
   sugar, sifted
 6 to 8 tablespoons milk
1½ teaspoons vanilla

Cream butter in a large bowl until fluffy. Blend in sugar a little at a time, alternating with a little of the milk. Stir in vanilla.

Rock Almond Topping

2 tablespoons butter *or*
  margarine
½ cup sugar
½ cup chopped almonds

Heat butter, sugar, and almonds in a large heavy skillet until golden brown, stirring occasionally. Set aside to cool.

Madeira Cake

¾ cup butter *or* margarine at room temperature
¾ cup sugar
1 teaspoon vanilla
 Zest of 1 lemon
3 eggs
2 cups flour
2 teaspoons baking powder
¼ teaspoon salt
½ cup milk
 Chocolate Glaze

Preheat oven to 350°. Grease and line a 9 x 5 x 3-inch loaf pan with waxed paper.

Cream butter in large bowl until fluffy. Sprinkle sugar over butter; mix well. Blend in vanilla and lemon zest. Add eggs, 1 at a time, beating well after each addition. Sift flour, baking powder, and salt together; add to batter, alternating with the milk. Stir until well blended.

Turn batter into prepared pan. Bake for 1 hour and 10 minutes or until a wooden skewer inserted in center comes out clean.

Cool cake in pan for 5 minutes; invert onto wire rack. Prepare Chocolate Glaze while cake is cooling. Drizzle glaze over cake.

Makes 8 to 10 servings

Chocolate Glaze

8 ounces semi-sweet chocolate
1 tablespoon butter *or* margarine

Melt chocolate and butter in top of double boiler over simmering water. Stir until blended.

Viennese Cake

6 eggs
1¾ cups light brown sugar
2 teaspoons vanilla
2½ cups flour
¼ cup cornstarch
2 teaspoons baking powder
¼ teaspoon salt
1¼ cups butter *or* margarine, melted
 Sweetened whipped cream

Preheat oven to 350°. Grease a 9-inch springform pan.

Beat eggs in a large bowl until fluffy. Sprinkle sugar over eggs; beat for 2 minutes. Blend in vanilla. Sift flour, cornstarch, baking powder, and salt together. Sprinkle flour mixture over batter; blend well. Stir in butter in a slow, steady stream; blend well.

Turn batter into prepared pan. Bake for 60 to 85 minutes or until a wooden skewer inserted in center comes out clean. Cool in pan for 5 minutes; invert onto wire rack. Cut into small slices; serve with sweetened whipped cream.

Makes 8 to 12 servings

Chocolate Loaf Cake

4 ounces semi-sweet chocolate
2 tablespoons butter *or* margarine
¾ cup butter *or* margarine at room temperature
1 cup sugar
1 teaspoon vanilla
2 tablespoons dark rum
4 eggs
2 cups flour
4 tablespoons cornstarch
1 teaspoon baking powder
1 cup blanched, ground almonds
¼ cup minced candied lemon peel
Confectioners' sugar

Preheat oven to 350°. Grease a 9 x 5 x 3-inch loaf pan.

Melt chocolate and 2 tablespoons butter in top of double boiler over simmering water. Stir to blend; set aside to cool. Cream remaining butter in large bowl until fluffy. Sprinkle sugar over butter; mix well. Blend in vanilla, rum, and chocolate mixture. Add eggs, 1 at a time, beating well after each addition. Sift flour, cornstarch, and baking powder together. Sprinkle flour mixture over batter; blend well. Stir in almonds and candied peel.

Turn batter into prepared pan. Bake 65 to 85 minutes or until a wooden skewer inserted in center comes out clean. Cool in pan for 5 minutes; invert onto wire rack. Sprinkle with confectioners' sugar.

Makes 8 servings

Pineapple Loaf

¾ cup almond paste
¾ cup butter *or* margarine at room temperature
¾ cup sugar
1 teaspoon vanilla
3 eggs
1¾ cups flour
2 teaspoons baking powder
¼ teaspoon salt
1 6-ounce can crushed pineapple, drained
8 ounces semi-sweet chocolate
1 tablespoon butter *or* margarine
Pineapple slices

Preheat oven to 375°. Grease a 9 x 5 x 3-inch loaf pan.

Cream almond paste and butter in large bowl. Gradually blend in sugar and vanilla. Add eggs, 1 at a time, beating well after each addition. Sift flour, baking powder, and salt together. Sprinkle flour mixture over batter; blend well. Stir crushed pineapple into batter.

Turn batter into prepared pan. Bake for 60 to 70 minutes or until wooden skewer inserted in center comes out clean. Cool in pan for 5 minutes; invert onto wire rack.

While cake is cooling, melt chocolate and butter in top of double boiler over simmering water. Stir to blend. Drizzle glaze over cooled cake; garnish with pineapple slices.

Makes 8 servings

Dundee Cake

1 cup butter *or* margarine at room temperature
1¼ cups sugar
4 eggs
2 cups flour
1 teaspoon baking powder
⅛ to ¼ cup milk
¾ cup dried currants, soaked and drained
¾ cup raisins
¼ cup candied cherries, cut in half
¼ cup candied orange peel *and/or* lemon peel
½ cup ground almonds
Zest of 1 orange
½ cup whole, blanched almonds

Preheat oven to 325°. Grease and line an 8-inch layer cake pan or springform pan with waxed paper.

Cream butter in large bowl until fluffy. Sprinkle sugar over butter; mix well. Add eggs, 1 at a time, beating well after each addition. Sift flour and baking powder together. Sprinkle over batter; blend well. Stir in just enough milk to make a smooth batter.

Gently fold in currants, raisins, cherries, candied peel, ground almonds and zest.

Spoon mixture into prepared pan. Place whole almonds in a circle on top of cake. Bake for 2½ hours or until center of the cake is firm and springy to the touch. Cool cake in pan. Place cake in an airtight container and store for 2 days before cutting and serving.

Makes 10 servings

Applesauce Spice Cake

1 cup butter *or* margarine at room temperature
2 cups sugar
1½ teaspoons ground cinnamon
½ teaspoon ground cloves
½ teaspoon allspice
¼ teaspoon ground nutmeg
¼ teaspoon salt
2 eggs
3 cups flour
2 teaspoons baking soda
2 cups unsweetened applesauce
1 cup golden raisins
1 cup dried currants, soaked and drained
¾ cup chopped walnuts *or* pecans

Preheat oven to 350°. Grease a 10-inch bundt pan or tube pan.

Cream butter in large bowl until fluffy. Sprinkle sugar over butter; mix well. Stir in spices. Add eggs, 1 at a time, beating well after each addition. Reserve ½ cup flour. Sift remaining 2½ cups flour and baking soda together; add to batter, alternating with applesauce. Blend well. Toss raisins, currants, and walnuts with remaining flour; blend into batter.

Turn batter into prepared pan. Bake for 50 to 55 minutes or until wooden skewer inserted in center come out clean. Cool cake in pan for 5 minutes. Invert cake onto wire rack and cool.

Makes 12 servings

Prince Regent Torte

1 cup butter *or* margarine at
    room temperature
1¼ cups sugar
1 teaspoon vanilla
4 eggs
1¾ cups flour
4 tablespoons cornstarch
1 teaspoon baking powder
¼ teaspoon salt
    Chocolate Buttercream
    Glaze
    Whipping cream, beaten
    stiff
    Chocolate wafers

Preheat oven to 375°. Cut out six 9-inch circles from waxed paper. Grease circles and place them on cookie sheets.

Cream butter in large bowl until fluffy. Sprinkle sugar over butter; mix well. Blend in vanilla. Add eggs, 1 at a time, beating well after each addition. Sift flour, cornstarch, baking powder, and salt together. Sprinkle flour mixture over batter; blend well.

Spoon batter onto circles. Position rack in center of oven; bake for 6 to 8 minutes or until layers are golden and spring back when lightly touched. Prepare Chocolate Buttercream while layers are baking. Invert layers onto a lightly floured surface. Sprinkle waxed paper lightly with water and remove. Turn layers upright onto wire rack to cool. Prepare Glaze while layers are cooling.

Trim layers with a sharp knife. Spread layers with Chocolate Buttercream, placing each atop the previous one on a cake plate. Spread top and sides of cake with remaining buttercream.

Drizzle Glaze over the top and sides of torte. Chill torte until Glaze is firm.

Before serving, fill a pastry bag fitted with a star tip with whipped cream, and pipe evenly spaced rosettes over torte. Garnish each rosette with a small chocolate wafer.

Makes 8 servings

Chocolate Buttercream

6 ounces semi-sweet
    chocolate
4 egg yolks
1 cup confectioners' sugar
1⅛ cups butter *or* margarine
    at room temperature
3 egg whites
¼ cup sugar

Melt chocolate in top of double boiler over simmering water; set aside to cool slightly. Combine egg yolks and confectioners' sugar in a small saucepan; arrange pan in top of double boiler over simmering water. Beat until thick; remove from heat. Set aside for 20 minutes, stirring occasionally. Beat in a small amount of butter at a time; continue beating until all the butter has been blended. Fold in melted chocolate.

Beat egg whites until soft peaks form. Sprinkle with ¼ cup sugar; continue beating until stiff peaks form. Fold egg whites into buttercream.

Glaze

6 ounces semi-sweet chocolate
1 tablespoon butter *or* margarine

Melt chocolate and butter in top of double boiler over simmering water. Stir until blended.

Macaroon Loaf

¾ cup butter *or* margarine at room temperature
¾ cup sugar
1 teaspoon vanilla
2 eggs
2 egg yolks
1⅓ cups flour
5 tablespoons cornstarch
1 teaspoon baking powder
¼ teaspoon salt
  Macaroon Filling

Preheat oven to 325°. Grease and line a 9 x 5 x 3-inch loaf pan with waxed paper.

Cream butter in large bowl until fluffy. Sprinkle sugar over butter; mix well. Blend in vanilla. Add eggs and egg yolks, 1 at a time, beating well after each addition. Sift flour, cornstarch, baking powder, and salt together. Sprinkle over batter a little at a time stirring until well blended.

Turn the dough into prepared pan. Prepare Macaroon Filling.

Using a spoon, make a long depression down the center of the dough, about 1½ inches deep and 1½ inches wide. Fill with Macaroon Filling.

Bake for 60 to 80 minutes or until a wooden skewer inserted in center comes out clean. Cool in pan for 5 minutes; invert onto wire rack.

Makes 8 to 10 servings

Macaroon Filling

2 egg whites
⅓ cup sugar
½ teaspoon vanilla
1 cup ground almonds

Beat egg whites in a bowl until soft peaks form. Add sugar and vanilla; beat until stiff peaks form. Fold in almonds.

Spritz Cookies

1 cup butter *or* margarine at
    room temperature
1 cup sugar
1 teaspoon vanilla
¼ teaspoon salt
½ cup blanched, ground
    almonds
2½ cups flour
1 rounded teaspoon cocoa,
    optional
1 rounded teaspoon sugar,
    optional

Preheat oven to 375°.

Cream butter in a large bowl until fluffy. Sprinkle sugar over butter; mix well. Blend in vanilla and salt. Sprinkle almonds and ⅔ the flour over batter; blend well. Knead the dough with the remaining flour on a pastry board.

If two-toned cookies are desired, remove ⅓ the dough and knead in cocoa and additional sugar. Pat out light dough with hands. Roll dark dough into a long strip; place in the middle of the light dough. Wrap the light dough around the dark dough.

Place dough in cookie press. Press cookies onto a 10 x 15-inch non-stick cookie sheet using different mold plates to form various shapes. Bake for 10 to 12 minutes or until golden. Remove from cookie sheet and cool on wire rack.

Makes 4 to 5 dozen

Pound Cake

¾ cup butter *or* margarine at
    room temperature
¾ cup sugar
1 teaspoon vanilla
4 eggs
2½ cups flour
1 teaspoon baking powder
¼ teaspoon salt
½ cup milk
¾ cup dried currants,
    soaked and drained
¾ cup raisins
2 cups confectioners' sugar,
    sifted
⅓ cup cocoa, sifted
6 tablespoons hot water
3 tablespoons butter *or*
    margarine, melted

Preheat oven to 275°. Grease a 9 x 5 x 3-inch loaf pan.

Cream butter in large bowl until fluffy. Sprinkle sugar over butter; mix well. Blend in vanilla. Add eggs, 1 at a time, beating well after each addition. Sift flour, baking powder, and salt together; add to batter, alternating with milk. Stir until well blended. Stir in currants and raisins.

Turn batter into prepared pan. Bake for 1½ hours or until a wooden skewer inserted in center comes out clean. Cool in pan 10 minutes; invert onto wire rack.

While cake is cooling, combine remaining ingredients in large bowl. Beat until smooth. Spread on cooled cake.

Makes 8 servings

Spritz Cookies, this page

Danube Waves

1 cup butter *or* margarine at room temperature
1 cup sugar
1 teaspoon vanilla
5 eggs
2½ cups flour
1 teaspoon baking powder
¼ teaspoon salt
2 teaspoons cocoa
2 to 4 tablespoons milk
1 17-ounce can pitted sour cherries, drained
Buttercream
Chocolate Glaze

Preheat oven to 350°. Grease and flour a 10 x 15-inch jelly-roll pan.

Cream butter in large bowl until fluffy. Sprinkle sugar over butter; mix well. Blend in vanilla. Add eggs, 1 at a time, beating well after each addition. Sift flour, baking powder, and salt together. Sprinkle flour mixture over batter; blend well.

Spread ⅔ of the dough in prepared pan. Combine cocoa and milk in a small bowl. Blend into remaining dough; mix well. Spread cocoa dough over dough on cookie sheet. Sprinkle cherries over dough.

Bake for 25 to 30 minutes or until a wooden skewer inserted in center comes out clean. While cake is baking, prepare Buttercream. Remove cake from oven and cool in pan for 5 minutes; invert onto wire rack.

Spread Buttercream over cooled cake. Set aside for 15 minutes. Prepare Chocolate Glaze. Cut cake into 2-inch squares. Drizzle squares with Chocolate Glaze.

Makes approximately 16 squares

Buttercream

¾ cup butter *or* margarine at room temperature
3½ to 4 cups confectioners' sugar
4 to 6 tablespoons milk
1 teaspoon vanilla

Cream butter in a large bowl until fluffy. Blend in sugar a little at a time, alternating with a little of the milk. Stir in vanilla.

Chocolate Glaze

8 ounces semi-sweet chocolate
1 tablespoon butter *or* margarine

Melt chocolate and butter in top of double boiler over simmering water. Stir to blend.

French Chocolate Cake

6 ounces semi-sweet
   chocolate
1 cup butter *or* margarine at
   room temperature,
   divided
1¼ cups sugar
1 teaspoon vanilla
6 eggs
2½ cups flour
2 teaspoons baking powder
¼ teaspoon salt
¾ cup blanched, ground
   almonds
   Apricot Glaze
   Chocolate Glaze
   Chopped pistachios

Preheat oven to 375°. Grease a 9 x 5 x 3-inch loaf pan.

Melt chocolate and ½ cup butter in top of double boiler over simmering water. Stir until blended; set aside to cool. Cream remaining butter in a large bowl until fluffy. Sprinkle sugar over butter; mix well. Blend in vanilla. Add eggs, 1 at a time, beating well after each addition. Blend in chocolate. Sift flour, baking powder, and salt together. Sprinkle flour mixture over batter; blend well. Stir in almonds.

Turn batter into prepared pan. Bake for 55 to 60 minutes or until a wooden skewer inserted in center comes out clean. Prepare Apricot Glaze while cake is baking; brush glaze on hot cake. Cool cake in pan on wire rack. Prepare Chocolate Glaze while cake is cooling. Drizzle on cooled cake; garnish with pistachios.

Makes 8 to 10 servings

Apricot Glaze

6 tablespoons apricot jam
2 tablespoons water

Heat apricot jam and water in saucepan over medium heat until smooth; mix well.

Chocolate Glaze

5 ounces semi-sweet
   chocolate
⅓ cup hot water

Melt chocolate in a small saucepan. Stir in hot water until well blended.

— Chocolate Almond Cake —

⅓ cup butter *or* margarine at
    room temperature
⅔ cup sugar
1 teaspoon vanilla
4 eggs
3 ounces semi-sweet
    chocolate, grated
⅓ cup flour
2 3½-ounce packages
    chocolate pudding mix
1½ teaspoons baking powder
¼ teaspoon salt
2 to 4 tablespoons milk
½ cup ground almonds
    Chocolate Glaze
⅓ cup chopped almonds

Preheat oven to 350°. Grease a 9 x 5 x 3-inch loaf pan.

Cream butter in large bowl until fluffy. Sprinkle with sugar; mix well. Blend in vanilla. Add eggs, 1 at a time, beating well after each addition. Stir in grated chocolate. Sift flour, pudding mix, baking powder and salt together. Add to batter a little at a time, alternating with milk until well blended. Fold in ground almonds.

Turn dough into prepared pan. Bake for 50 to 60 minutes or until a wooden skewer inserted in center comes out clean. Cool in pan for 5 minutes; invert onto wire rack.

Prepare Chocolate Glaze while cake is cooling. Drizzle glaze over top and sides of cake. Garnish with chopped almonds.

Makes 8 to 10 servings

—————— Chocolate Glaze ——————

4 ounces semi-sweet
    chocolate
1 tablespoon butter *or*
    margarine

Melt chocolate and butter in top of double boiler over simmering water. Stir until blended.

— Ice Cream Wafer Cones —

½ cup butter *or* margarine at
    room temperature
1¼ cups sugar
1 teaspoon vanilla
2 eggs
1¾ cups flour
¼ teaspoon salt
2 cups milk
    Ice cream *or* sweetened
    whipped cream

Cream butter in large bowl until fluffy. Sprinkle sugar over butter; mix well. Blend in vanilla. Add eggs, 1 at a time, beating well after each addition. Sift flour and salt together; add to batter, alternating with milk until well blended.

Preheat waffle iron. Ladle batter onto hot iron. Cook wafers until golden. Remove from iron and roll into cones while still hot. Set aside to cool.

Store in containers with tight-fitting lids. To serve, fill with ice cream or whipped cream.

Makes approximately 10 cones

Hazelnut Buns

½ cup butter *or* margarine at
    room temperature
¾ cup sugar
1 teaspoon vanilla
2 eggs
1½ cups flour
½ teaspoon baking powder
¼ teaspoon salt
1¼ cups ground hazelnuts
    Light Glaze

Preheat oven to 350°. Grease a 10 x 15-inch cookie sheet.

Cream butter in a large bowl until fluffy. Sprinkle sugar over butter; mix well. Blend in vanilla. Add eggs, 1 at a time, beating well after each addition. Sift flour, baking powder, and salt together. Sprinkle flour mixture over batter; blend well. Stir in hazelnuts.

Place dough in a pastry bag. Pipe walnut-sized mounds of batter onto prepared cookie sheet. Bake 10 to 15 minutes or until golden. Cool on cookie sheet. While buns are cooling, prepare Light Glaze. Drizzle glaze over buns.

Makes 8 servings

Light Glaze

1¼ cups confectioners' sugar
1 to 2 egg whites

Place sugar in mixing bowl. Stir in enough egg white to make a smooth spreadable consistency.

Cream Waffles

½ cup butter *or* margarine at
    room temperature
½ cup sugar
1 teaspoon vanilla
4 egg yolks
1¾ cups flour
4 tablespoons cornstarch
1½ teaspoons baking powder
¼ teaspoon salt
1 cup whipping cream
4 egg whites
    Confectioners' sugar

Grease waffle iron, if desired, and preheat.

Cream butter in large bowl until fluffy. Sprinkle sugar over butter; mix well. Blend in vanilla. Add egg yolks, 1 at a time, beating well after each addition. Sift flour, cornstarch, baking powder, and salt together. Add to batter, a little at a time, alternating with cream; stir until well blended. Beat egg whites until stiff but not dry. Fold egg whites into batter.

Ladle batter onto waffle iron according to manufacturer's directions. Cook until golden brown. Invert onto wire rack; sprinkle with confectioners' sugar.

Makes 8 to 10 servings

Apple Flan

½ cup butter *or* margarine at room temperature
¾ cup sugar
1 teaspoon vanilla
3 eggs
2 cups flour
2 teaspoons baking powder
¼ teaspoon salt
4 tablespoons milk
1½ pounds firm cooking apples, peeled and halved
6 tablespoons apricot jam
3 tablespoons water

Preheat oven to 375°. Grease a deep 9-inch pie plate or flan pan.

Cream butter in large bowl until fluffy. Sprinkle sugar over butter; mix well. Blend in vanilla. Add eggs, 1 at a time, beating well after each addition. Sift flour, baking powder, and salt together; add to batter, alternating with milk. Stir until well blended.

Turn batter into prepared pan. Cut each apple half into a fan shape; arrange decoratively over batter. Bake 45 to 50 minutes or until golden. Invert onto wire rack.

While flan is baking, heat apricot jam and water in a small saucepan. Cook over medium heat until mixture begins to boil. Stir to blend; brush glaze over warm flan.

Makes 8 servings

Moorland Sweet Cookies

1 cup butter *or* margarine
1 cup sugar
¼ cup milk
1 teaspoon vanilla
3 cups flour
1 teaspoon baking powder
¼ teaspoon salt

Preheat oven to 375°. Line a 10 x 15-inch cookie sheet with waxed paper.

Melt butter in small saucepan, just until it begins to brown, then chill until firm. Cream butter in a large bowl until fluffy. Sprinkle sugar over butter; mix well. Blend in milk and vanilla. Sift flour, baking powder, and salt together. Sprinkle ⅔ the flour mixture over batter; blend until dough begins to cling together.

Turn out dough onto lightly floured board. Knead with remaining flour until a smooth dough is formed. Shape dough into two 12-inch rolls. Cover with plastic wrap; chill until firm.

Slice rolls approximately ½ inch thick. Arrange slices on cookie sheet. Bake for 10 to 15 minutes or until golden. Cool on cookie sheet.

Makes 8 to 10 servings

Apple Flan, this page

Marzipan Sticks

¾ cup almond paste at room temperature
½ cup butter *or* margarine at room temperature
½ cup sugar
1 teaspoon vanilla
Zest of 1 lemon
2 eggs
1¾ cups flour
1 teaspoon baking powder
¼ teaspoon salt
4 ounces semi-sweet chocolate
1 tablespoon butter *or* margarine

Preheat oven to 375°. Line a 10 x 15-inch cookie sheet with parchment paper or foil.

Crumble almond paste into large bowl. Cream paste and ½ cup butter until smooth. Blend in sugar, vanilla, and zest. Add eggs, 1 at a time, beating well after each addition. Sift flour, baking powder, and salt together. Sprinkle flour mixture over batter; blend well.

Place dough in a pastry bag fitted with a small, plain tip. Pipe out 2-inch long spirals or straight sticks onto prepared cookie sheet. Bake for 8 to 10 minutes or until golden. Cool in pan for 5 minutes. Place on wire rack.

While marzipan sticks are cooling, melt chocolate and remaining butter in top of double boiler over simmering water. Stir until blended. Dip one end of each cooled marzipan stick into the chocolate, coating half the stick. Place on waxed paper to dry.

Makes 8 to 10 servings

King's Loaf

1 cup butter *or* margarine at room temperature
1 cup sugar
2 tablespoons dark rum
1 teaspoon vanilla
5 eggs
3½ cups flour
2 teaspoons baking powder
¼ teaspoon salt
½ cup milk
¾ cup dried currants, soaked and drained
¾ cup raisins
¾ cup chopped candied citron

Preheat oven to 350°. Grease a 9 x 5 x 3-inch loaf pan or a 10-inch tube pan; line bottom with waxed paper.

Cream butter in large bowl until fluffy. Sprinkle sugar over butter; mix well. Blend in rum and vanilla. Add eggs, 1 at a time, beating well after each addition. Reserve ¼ cup flour. Sift remaining flour, baking powder, and salt together; add to batter alternating with milk. Stir until thick and well blended. Toss currants, raisins, and candied peel in reserved flour; fold into batter.

Turn batter into prepared pan. Bake for 1 hour and 20 minutes or until a wooden skewer inserted in center comes out clean. Cool in pan for 10 minutes; invert onto wire rack. Cut into small slices.

Makes 10 to 12 servings

English Loaf Cake

½ cup butter *or* margarine at room temperature
¾ cup sugar
1 teaspoon vanilla
Zest of ½ lemon
2 eggs
2 cups flour
2 teaspoons baking powder
¼ teaspoon salt
½ cup heavy cream
¾ cup raisins
¾ cup dried currants, soaked and drained
¼ cup diced candied lemon peel
¼ cup sliced candied cherries

Preheat oven to 350°. Grease and line a 9 x 5 x 3-inch loaf pan with waxed paper.

Cream butter in large bowl until fluffy. Sprinkle sugar over butter; mix well. Blend in vanilla and lemon zest. Add eggs, 1 at a time, beating well after each addition. Reserving ¼ cup flour, sift remaining flour, baking powder, and salt together. Sprinkle flour mixture over batter; blend well. Stir in heavy cream. Toss fruit with reserved flour; fold into batter.

Turn batter into prepared pan. Bake about 55 to 65 minutes or until a wooden skewer inserted in center comes out clean.

Cool in pan for 5 minutes; invert onto wire rack.

Note: The cake can be covered in plastic wrap and stored at room temperature for several days, refrigerated, or frozen.

Makes 8 to 10 servings

Creme de Cacao Cake

¼ cup butter *or* margarine at room temperature
1¼ cups sugar
2 tablespoons creme de cacao liqueur, *or* to taste
1 teaspoon chocolate extract
1 teaspoon vanilla
3 eggs
1¾ cups flour
½ cup cocoa
1½ teaspoons baking powder
½ teaspoon salt
1 cup sour cream
Confectioners' sugar

Preheat oven to 325°. Grease and line a 9 x 5 x 3-inch loaf pan with waxed paper.

Cream butter in large bowl until fluffy. Sprinkle sugar over butter; mix well. Blend in creme de cacao, chocolate extract, and vanilla. Add eggs, 1 at a time, beating well after each addition. Sift flour, cocoa, baking powder, and salt together; add to batter, alternating with sour cream. Stir until well blended.

Turn batter into prepared pan. Bake for 1¼ hours or until a wooden skewer inserted in center comes out clean. Cool cake in pan for 5 minutes. Invert onto rack; cool. Sprinkle with confectioners' sugar.

Makes 6 to 8 servings

Banana Cake

¾ cup butter *or* margarine at room temperature
1½ cups sugar
1 teaspoon vanilla
½ teaspoon ground cinnamon
½ teaspoon salt
2 eggs
2 medium to large bananas, mashed
2 cups flour
1 teaspoon baking powder
1 teaspoon baking soda
¾ cup buttermilk
½ cup chopped walnuts
2 egg whites
1½ cups butter *or* margarine at room temperature
1½ teaspoons vanilla
4 cups confectioners' sugar, sifted

Preheat oven to 375°. Grease two 8-inch layer cake pans.

Cream butter in large bowl until fluffy. Sprinkle sugar over butter; mix well. Blend in vanilla, cinnamon, and salt. Add eggs, 1 at a time, beating well after each addition. Blend in mashed bananas. Sift flour, baking powder, and baking soda together; add to batter, alternating with buttermilk. Stir until well blended. Blend in walnuts.

Turn batter into prepared pans. Bake for 20 to 25 minutes or until a wooden skewer inserted in center comes out clean. Cool in pan for 5 minutes. Invert onto wire rack; cool.

While cakes are cooling, beat egg whites and butter in large bowl until fluffy. Blend in vanilla. Sprinkle confectioners' sugar over mixture; beat until creamy and light.

Place bottom cake layer on a serving plate; spread with frosting mixture. Place remaining layer on top; spread top and sides of cake with remaining frosting.

Makes 8 servings

Cream Slices

½ cup butter *or* margarine at room temperature
½ cup sugar
1 teaspoon vanilla
Zest of ½ lemon
2 eggs
1½ cups flour
1 teaspoon baking powder
¼ teaspoon salt
½ cup ground almonds
Raspberry Buttercream
Raspberry jam

Preheat oven to 375°. Grease a 10 x 15-inch jelly-roll pan.

Cream butter in a large bowl until fluffy. Sprinkle sugar over butter; mix well. Blend in vanilla and lemon zest. Add eggs, 1 at a time, beating well after each addition. Sift flour, baking powder, and salt together. Sprinkle flour mixture over batter; blend well. Stir in ground almonds.

With floured hands, pat dough into prepared pan. Loosely arrange a sheet of foil over dough. Bake for 15 to 20 minutes or until a wooden skewer inserted in center comes out clean. Cool on wire rack. Prepare Raspberry Buttercream while cake is cooling.

Cut cake down the middle. Spread one half of the cake lightly with raspberry jam. Arrange remaining half on top. If necessary, cut the edges to align cake. Frost cake with Raspberry Buttercream. Cut into 1 x 3-inch slices.

Makes approximately 2 dozen

Raspberry Buttercream

¾ cup butter *or* margarine at room temperature
3½ to 4 cups confectioners' sugar, sifted
1 to 2 tablespoons milk
3 to 4 tablespoons raspberry liqueur

Cream butter in a large bowl until fluffy. Blend in sugar a little at a time, alternating with the liquids.

Orange Pound Cake

½ cup butter *or* margarine at room temperature
1 cup sugar, divided
1 teaspoon vanilla
Zest of 1 orange, divided
3 eggs
2 cups flour
2 teaspoons baking powder
¼ teaspoon salt
½ cup orange juice
Confectioners' sugar

Preheat oven to 375°. Grease a 9 x 5 x 3-inch loaf pan.

Cream butter in large bowl until fluffy. Sprinkle ¾ cup sugar over butter; mix well. Blend in vanilla, and ½ the orange zest. Add eggs, 1 at a time, beating well after each addition. Sift flour, baking powder, and salt together. Sprinkle flour mixture over batter; blend well.

Turn batter into prepared pan. Bake for 35 to 45 minutes or until a wooden skewer inserted in center comes out clean.

While cake is baking, combine orange juice, remaining zest, and remaining sugar in a small saucepan. Place over medium heat until mixture begins to boil, stirring often. Remove from heat.

Remove cake from pan and place on wire rack over a plate.

Prick warm cake with fork; sprinkle with juice mixture. Repeat process until all the juice has been absorbed. Sprinkle cake with confectioners' sugar. Cool before serving.

Makes 8 servings

Marbled Pound Cake

1¼ cups butter *or* margarine
    at room temperature
1½ cups sugar, divided
 1 teaspoon vanilla
 5 eggs
 3 cups flour
 2 teaspoons baking powder
 ¼ teaspoon salt
 ¼ to ⅓ cup milk
 ½ cup cocoa, sifted
 6 tablespoons milk
    Confectioners' sugar

Preheat oven to 375°. Grease a 10-inch bundt pan.

Cream butter in large bowl until fluffy. Sprinkle 1¼ cups sugar over butter; mix well. Blend in vanilla. Add eggs, 1 at a time, beating well after each addition. Sift flour, baking powder, and salt together; add to batter, alternating with enough milk to form a smooth dough.

Pour ⅔ of the batter into prepared bundt pan. Blend cocoa, ¼ cup sugar, and 6 tablespoons milk into remaining batter; mix well. Drop mixture by the tablespoonful onto batter. Using a knife, gently swirl cocoa mixture through the batter to make a marbled design.

Bake for 50 to 65 minutes or until a wooden skewer inserted in the center comes out clean. Cool cake in pan for 5 minutes; invert onto wire rack. Sprinkle with confectioners' sugar.

Makes 12 to 14 servings

Creamy Nutcakes

 1 8-ounce package nutcake
    mix with icing
 ⅓ cup margarine at room
    temperature
 2 eggs
 5 tablespoons water
 1 1-pound jar stewed
    apricots, drained and
    juice reserved
 1 cup ground walnuts
 2 tablespoons half-and-half
 ½ cup whipping cream
    Chocolate curls

Preheat oven to 350°.

Prepare cake mix using margarine, egg, and water according to package directions. Stir in half the icing mix.

Place paper cupcake liners in muffin tin. Fill each cup about ⅓ full with batter. Bake for 30 minutes or until a wooden skewer inserted in center comes out clean.

Bring reserved apricot juice to a boil in a small saucepan. Pierce cupcakes with a fork several times. Pour apricot juice over cupcakes. Top each with an apricot. Combine nuts and half-and-half in a bowl; stir in remaining icing mix. Whip cream until stiff; fold into nut mixture.

Pipe mounds of whipped cream mixture on top of apricots. Garnish with chocolate curls.

Makes 10 to 12 servings

Marbled Pound Cake, this page

Butter Ropes

1 cup plus 1 tablespoon
   butter *or* margarine at
   room temperature
⅔ cup sugar
8 egg yolks, divided
   Zest of 1 lemon
3 cups flour.

Cream butter in large bowl until fluffy. Sprinkle sugar over butter; mix well. Add 6 egg yolks, 1 at a time, beating well after each addition. Blend in lemon zest. Sprinkle flour over batter; blend well. Shape dough into a ball. Flatten slightly and cover with plastic wrap. Refrigerate for 1 hour.

Preheat oven to 350°.

Working with about ⅓ of the dough at a time, roll each piece into a 1½-inch log on a lightly floured surface. Cut into ½-inch slices. Roll each slice into a 4-inch rope. Shape ropes into the letter "S."

Place ropes on a 10 x 15-inch non-stick cookie sheet. Beat remaining 2 egg yolks and brush over cookies. Sprinkle with sugar.

Bake for 12 to 15 minutes or until edges are golden brown. Cool slightly on cookie sheet. Place on wire rack to cool completely.

Makes approximately 6 dozen

Orange Rum Cake

2⅔ cups cake flour
2½ teaspoons baking powder
½ teaspoon salt
¼ teaspoon baking soda
⅛ teaspoon ginger
⅔ cup butter *or* margarine at
   room temperature
1⅓ cups sugar
3 egg yolks
1½ teaspoons orange zest
¾ cup orange juice
⅓ cup rum
½ teaspoon almond extract
½ teaspoon vanilla
3 egg whites, beaten stiff
   Confectioners' sugar

Preheat oven to 350°. Grease a 10-inch tube pan.

Sift together first 5 ingredients twice. Set aside. Cream butter in large bowl until fluffy. Sprinkle sugar over butter; mix well. Add egg yolks, 1 at a time, beating well after each addition. Blend in orange zest. Add flour mixture to batter, alternating with orange juice and rum. Blend well. Stir in almond extract and vanilla. Fold in beaten egg whites.

Turn batter into prepared pan. Bake for 45 to 60 minutes or until a wooden skewer inserted in center comes out clean. Cool in pan for 15 minutes; loosen edges with knife. Invert onto wire rack to cool.

Sprinkle with confectioners' sugar before serving.

Makes 12 to 14 servings

Lemon Pound Cake

1 cup butter *or* margarine at room temperature
1¼ cups sugar
4 large eggs at room temperature
Zest of 1 lemon
2 cups flour
2 teaspoons baking powder

Preheat oven to 350°. Grease and flour a 9 x 5 x 3-inch loaf pan.

Cream butter in large bowl until fluffy. Sprinkle sugar over butter; mix well. Add eggs, 1 at a time, beating well after each addition. Blend in lemon zest. Sift flour and baking powder together. Sprinkle over batter, a bit at a time; blend well.

Turn batter into prepared pan. Bake for 1 hour or until a wooden skewer inserted in center comes out clean.

Cool cake completely in pan placed on wire rack.

Makes 10 to 12 servings

Walnut Roll-Ups

½ cup butter *or* margarine at room temperature
4 ounces cream cheese at room temperature
1 cup flour
1 tablespoon sugar
¼ teaspoon salt
Zest of ½ lemon
1½ cups ground walnuts
⅓ cup sugar
⅓ cup whipping cream
1½ tablespoons dark rum
½ cup confectioners' sugar
1 teaspoon lemon juice
2 teaspoons water

Cream butter and cream cheese in a large bowl until fluffy. Add flour, 1 tablespoon sugar, salt, and lemon zest; mix until dough holds together. Shape into a 6 or 7-inch block. Wrap in plastic wrap; refrigerate overnight.

Preheat oven to 375°. Divide dough into two parts. Roll out each part on a lightly floured board into a 13 x 4-inch rectangle. Combine nuts, ⅓ cup sugar, cream, and rum; blend well. Spread nut mixture over dough to within ½ inch of the edges. Roll up dough from opposite sides toward the center. Lightly pinch center seam together.

Place rolls, seam sides down, on a 10 x 15-inch non-stick cookie sheet. Bake for 30 minutes or until golden. Cool in pan on wire rack for 10 minutes. Remove rolls from pan; cool completely on wire rack.

In a small bowl, blend confectioners' sugar, lemon juice, and water until smooth. Spread over rolls. Cut into 1-inch slices.

Makes approximately 24

Rhubarb Crumble

¼ cup butter *or* margarine
¼ cup sugar
1 teaspoon vanilla
1 egg
2 cups flour
2 teaspoons baking powder
¼ teaspoon salt
½ cup milk
2 pounds rhubarb, cleaned,
 drained and cut into
 2-inch pieces (*or* other
 fruit of the season)
½ cup sugar
3 egg whites
¾ cup sugar

Preheat oven to 375°. Grease a 10-inch pie pan.

Cream butter in large bowl until fluffy. Sprinkle ¼ cup sugar over butter; mix well. Blend in vanilla and egg. Sift flour, baking powder, and salt together; add to batter, alternating with milk. Stir until blended; batter will be stiff.

Turn batter into prepared pie pan. Arrange rhubarb over dough. Sprinkle with ½ cup sugar. Bake for 25 to 30 minutes or until a wooden skewer inserted in center comes out clean.

While cake is baking, beat egg whites until soft peaks form. Sprinkle remaining sugar over egg whites ¼ cup at a time; continue beating until stiff but not dry peaks form. Preheat oven to 400°.

Mound meringue over rhubarb, spreading it smoothly to seal the edges. Bake for 8 minutes or until lightly browned. Slice and serve while warm.

Makes 8 servings

Fig Buns

1 9-ounce packaged fruit
 cake mix
½ cup margarine at room
 temperature
1 egg
2 tablespoons milk
½ pound fresh figs, peeled
 and chopped *or* chopped
 dried dates
 Apricot Glaze
 Sugar

Preheat oven to 375°. Grease a 10 x 15-inch cookie sheet.

Prepare fruit cake according to package directions using margarine, egg, and milk.

Place dough into a pastry bag fitted with a star tip. Pipe spirals onto prepared cookie sheet. Arrange figs on top of spirals. Bake for 15 minutes or until golden. Prepare Apricot Glaze.

Place buns on serving platter and brush with glaze. Sprinkle with sugar.

Makes 10 to 12 servings

Cocoa Layer Cake

6 tablespoons butter *or* margarine at room temperature
1 cup firmly packed light brown sugar
½ cup sugar
1½ teaspoons vanilla
3 eggs
2 cups flour
1 teaspoon baking soda
¼ teaspoon salt
½ cup cocoa
1 cup buttermilk
 Cocoa Frosting

Preheat oven to 350°. Grease two 9-inch layer cake pans.

Cream butter in large bowl until fluffy. Sprinkle both sugars over butter; mix well. Blend in vanilla. Add eggs, 1 at a time, beating well after each addition. Sift flour, baking soda, salt, and cocoa together; add to batter, alternating with buttermilk. Stir until well blended.

Turn batter evenly into cake pans. Bake for 20 minutes or until a wooden skewer inserted in center comes out clean. Cool cakes in pan for 5 minutes; invert onto wire rack. Prepare Cocoa Frosting while cakes are cooling.

Place 1 cake layer on serving plate. Spread with frosting. Place remaining layer on top; spread top and sides of cake with remaining frosting. Chill cake until ready to serve.

Makes 8 to 10 servings

Cocoa Frosting

3 egg whites
¼ teaspoon salt
⅓ cup sugar
¾ cup light corn syrup
1½ teaspoons vanilla
2 tablespoons cocoa, sifted

Beat egg whites and salt in large bowl until soft peaks form. Sprinkle sugar, 1 tablespoonful at a time, over egg whites, beating well after each addition. Continue beating until all the sugar has been used. Pour in corn syrup in a slow, steady stream while beating; continue to beat egg whites until stiff peaks form. Sprinkle vanilla and cocoa over mixture; blend well.

Fruit Flan

¼ cup butter *or* margarine at
    room temperature
2 tablespoons vegetable
    shortening
2 teaspoons sugar
1½ cups flour
¼ teaspoon salt
6 to 8 tablespoons ice water
3 cups sliced or whole
    mixed fruit of your choice
¾ cup currant jelly
6 tablespoons water

Preheat oven to 400°. Use a 9 or 9½-inch flan pan with removable bottom.

Cream butter and shortening in large bowl until fluffy. Sprinkle sugar over butter; mix well. Sift flour with salt. Sprinkle flour over batter; blend well. Sprinkle water over dough, 1 tablespoonful at a time, and mix until dough holds together. Shape into a ball; cover with plastic wrap. Chill for 15 minutes.

Roll out dough to form a 10-inch circle. Place in pan; trim. Line pastry shell with aluminum foil and fill with pastry weights or dried beans. Bake for 12 minutes. Remove weights and foil. Prick flan and continue baking for 6 to 8 minutes or until flan is golden brown. Invert and cool on wire rack.

When ready to serve. arrange fruit decoratively over flan shell. Combine currant jelly and water in a small saucepan; heat on medium until mixture begins to boil. Stir until blended; brush glaze over fruit using a pastry brush.

Makes 6 to 8 servings

Pecan Pound Cake

1 cup butter *or* margarine at
    room temperature
2¾ cups sugar
1 teaspoon vanilla
3 cups flour
¼ teaspoon baking soda
½ teaspoon salt
1 cup sour cream
1 cup ground pecans

Preheat oven to 350°. Grease and line a 10-inch tube pan with waxed paper.

Cream butter in large bowl until fluffy. Sprinkle sugar over butter; mix well. Blend in vanilla. Sift flour, baking soda, and salt together; add to batter, alternating with sour cream. Stir until well blended.

Sprinkle pecans over the bottom of prepared pan. Turn batter into pan; bake for 1 hour and 20 minutes or until a wooden skewer inserted in center comes out clean. Cool in pan on rack. Remove from pan and discard paper.

Makes 10 to 12 servings

Orange & Chocolate Cake

4 ounces semi-sweet
  chocolate
1 ounce unsweetened
  chocolate
½ cup butter *or* margarine at
  room temperature
¾ cup sugar, divided
4 eggs, separated
2 tablespoons orange
  liqueur
1 cup sifted cake flour
  Orange Buttercream
  Orange and Chocolate
  Glaze

Preheat oven to 350°. Grease and flour an 8-inch cake pan with removable bottom.

Melt both chocolates in the top of a double boiler over simmering water; set aside. Cream butter in large bowl until fluffy. Sprinkle all but 2 tablespoons sugar over butter; mix well. Add egg yolks, 1 at a time, beating well after each addition. Blend in melted chocolate and liqueur.

Beat egg whites in a small bowl until soft peaks form. Gradually add remaining 2 tablespoons sugar; beat until stiff peaks form. Fold about ¼ of the egg whites into chocolate mixture, then alternate folding in flour and remaining whites.

Turn batter into prepared pan. Bake for 30 minutes or until a wooden skewer inserted in center comes out clean. Cool in pan on a wire rack for about 15 minutes. Loosen edge of cake; remove rim from pan. Do not remove bottom of pan. Cool completely on wire rack. While cake is cooling, prepare Orange Buttercream.

Place cake, still on pan bottom, on a serving plate. Spread Orange Buttercream over entire cake. Refrigerate until buttercream is very firm, or place cake in freezer until set.

Prepare Orange and Chocolate Glaze. Drizzle glaze over top of cake. Use a metal spatula to spread glaze evenly. Refrigerate until set.

Makes 8 to 10 servings

Orange Buttercream

1 egg yolk
⅓ cup confectioners' sugar
5 tablespoons butter *or*
  margarine at room
  temperature
1½ tablespoons orange
  liqueur

Beat egg yolk and confectioners' sugar in a double boiler over simmering water until thick and light-colored. Remove from heat. Beat until lukewarm. Gradually beat in butter. Blend in liqueur.

Orange and Chocolate Glaze

2 ounces semi-sweet
  chocolate
1 tablespoon orange liqueur
¼ cup butter *or* margarine at
  room temperature

Melt chocolate and liqueur in a double boiler over simmering water. Gradually blend in butter. Remove from heat. Let stand, stirring often, until chocolate begins to thicken but is still of pouring consistency.

Coconut Lemon Ring

¾ cup butter *or* margarine at
  room temperature
1 cup sugar
4 eggs, separated
  Zest of 1 lemon
1½ cups flour
1½ teaspoons baking powder
2 tablespoons milk
½ cup shredded coconut
  Lemon Glaze

Preheat oven to 350°. Grease and flour an 8-inch tube pan with a removable bottom.

Cream butter in large bowl until fluffy. Sprinkle sugar over butter; mix well. Add egg yolks, 1 at a time, beating well after each addition. Blend in lemon zest. Sift flour and baking powder together. Sprinkle flour mixture over batter; blend well. Stir in milk and coconut.

Beat egg whites in a small bowl until stiff peaks form. Stir about ¼ the egg whites into the batter. Gently fold in remaining egg whites.

Turn batter into prepared pan. Bake for 1 hour or until a wooden skewer inserted in the center comes out clean. Cool cake completely in pan on a wire rack. Loosen edge of cake from pan. Remove rim and pan bottom. Place cake on a serving plate.

Prepare Lemon Glaze while cake is cooling. Drizzle glaze over cake.

Makes 16 servings

Lemon Glaze

1 cup confectioners' sugar,
  sifted
2 tablespoons lemon juice
3 tablespoons butter,
  melted

Combine confectioners' sugar, lemon juice, and melted butter in a small bowl; blend until smooth. Let glaze stand for 3 to 4 minutes to thicken.

Tangy Fruit Cake

½ cup butter *or* margarine at room temperature
¾ cup sugar
2 eggs
1 tablespoon lemon zest
1 teaspoon lemon extract
1⅔ cups cake flour
1½ teaspoons baking powder
¼ teaspoon salt
⅔ cup milk
  Confectioners' sugar
  Sliced and sweetened strawberries
1 cup whipping cream, whipped

Preheat oven to 325°. Grease and flour a 6½-cup ring mold.

Cream butter in large bowl until fluffy. Sprinkle sugar over butter; mix well. Add eggs, 1 at a time, beating well after each addition. Blend in lemon zest and extract. Sift flour, baking powder, and salt together; add to batter, alternating with milk. Blend well.

Turn batter into prepared mold. Bake for 30 to 40 minutes or until a wooden skewer inserted in center comes out clean. Cool in pan for 10 minutes. Invert cake onto rack to cool completely.

Place cake on serving plate. Sprinkle with confectioners' sugar. Fill center with strawberries and top with whipped cream.

Makes 10 to 12 servings

Wellesley Fudge Cake

3 ounces unsweetened chocolate
½ cup butter *or* margarine at room temperature
2 cups firmly packed brown sugar
2 eggs
1 teaspoon vanilla
½ cup milk
½ cup water
½ cup flour
1 teaspoon baking soda
½ teaspoon salt
  Fudge Icing

Preheat oven to 350°. Grease and flour two 9-inch cake pans.

Melt chocolate in double boiler over simmering water; set aside. Cream butter in large bowl until fluffy. Sprinkle sugar over butter; mix well. Add eggs, 1 at a time, beating well after each addition. Blend in vanilla and melted chocolate. Combine milk and water; set aside. Sift flour, baking soda, and salt together; add to batter, alternating with milk mixture. Blend well.

Turn batter into prepared pans. Bake for 30 to 35 minutes or until a wooden skewer inserted in center comes out clean. Cool in pan for 5 minutes; invert cakes onto wire racks and cool completely. Prepare Fudge Icing while cakes are cooling.

Place one layer on serving plate; frost top of layer. Place second layer atop the other. Frost top and sides of cake.

Makes 12 servings

Fudge Icing

2 cups firmly packed brown
  sugar
½ cup milk
3 ounces semi-sweet
  chocolate, melted
2 tablespoons butter *or*
  margarine at room
  temperature

Combine sugar and milk in small bowl; stir in melted chocolate and butter until mixture is well blended.

Broiled Layer Cake

1 cup butter *or* margarine at
  room temperature
1¼ cups sugar
1 teaspoon vanilla
2 eggs
4 egg yolks
1½ cups flour
4 tablespoons cornstarch
1 tablespoon baking
  powder
¼ teaspoon salt
4 egg whites
4 ounces semi-sweet
  chocolate
1 tablespoon butter *or*
  margarine
  Sweetened whipped
  cream

Preheat broiler. Grease a 9 x 5 x 3-inch loaf pan; line with greased waxed paper.

Cream butter in large bowl until fluffy. Sprinkle sugar over butter; mix well. Blend in vanilla. Add eggs and yolks, 1 at a time, beating well after each addition. Sift flour, cornstarch, baking powder, and salt together. Sprinkle flour mixture over batter; blend well. Beat egg whites until stiff but not dry. Fold egg whites into batter.

Spread thin layer of batter in bottom of prepared pan. Broil 2 minutes or until lightly browned, 7 to 8 inches from the heat if possible. Repeat steps until all the dough has been used. If possible, lower oven rack so that each new layer is also 7 to 8 inches from heat.

Carefully loosen finished cake with a knife. Turn cake out onto cookie sheet. Sprinkle waxed paper lightly with water and remove. Return cake to hot oven for 5 minutes. Cool.

While cake is cooling, melt chocolate and butter in top of double boiler over simmering water. Stir until blended. Drizzle glaze over cooled cake. Slice cake thinly and serve with sweetened whipped cream.

Makes 8 to 10 servings

Tortes, Gateaux, and Cake Rolls

Many of the recipes in this chapter are made without butter. The main ingredients of cakes baked without butter are eggs, sugar, and flour. Beaten eggs give these sponge-type cakes their light, fluffy texture. The air beaten into the eggs and the steam created during baking cause the cake to rise. These delicate, golden cakes are excellent for filling and decorating to create beautiful and elaborate desserts such as gateaux, tortes, and fancy, rolled cakes.

Tortes, Gateaux, and Cake Rolls

Important Preparations

1 Line the base of the jelly-roll pans or cake pans.

2 Trace the bottom of the pan onto the waxed paper.

3 Cut out the tracing.

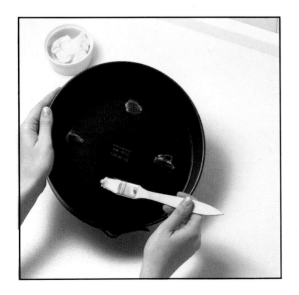

1 Grease the bottom of the pan with butter or margarine.

2 Brush butter or margarine on the bottom of the pan in several places.

3 **Do not** grease the sides of the pan as this will keep the cake from rising.

1 Place the waxed paper in the bottom of the pan.

2 Press firmly into place.

3 Smooth the paper until there are no bumps or folds and the paper lies firmly in place.

4 If you do not use waxed paper, **do not** grease the bottom of the pan.

The Individual Steps

1 Check the eggs for freshness. The fresher the eggs, the lighter and airier the texture will be.

2 Break each egg into a cup before adding to the mixing bowl to be sure it is good.

1 A tablespoon of water may be added when beating eggs. Some cooks prefer to add a small amount of water when beating eggs to increase the volume if eggs are small.

2 Beat the eggs until they are light and fluffy.

1 Add the sugar and vanilla and any spices called for in the recipe.

2 Sprinkle the sugar and vanilla over the eggs.

3 Beat for 2 minutes.

4 Add any spices or flavorings called for; blend well.

1 Sift the flour and any other dry ingredients together. Sifting the flour helps to remove any lumps and helps to evenly distribute the other dry ingredients throughout the flour.

2 Sprinkle the dry ingredients over the eggs a little at a time.

3 Use a mixer or fold in with a spatula only until well blended.

1 Turn the batter into the prepared cake pan.

2 Use a rubber spatula to spread the batter evenly in the pan.

Baking

A sponge-type cake should be baked immediately after being prepared so it will not lose any of its air and collapse. Follow instructions for baking the proper amount of time. Before removing the cake from the oven, always check to see if it is done by gently pressing on it with your fingertips. The cake should spring back when lightly touched. It should not feel moist, but should be soft and spongy. An overbaked sponge cake will feel dry and hard. Remove from oven and cool for 5 to 10 minutes in pan before decorating or filling.

1 When the sponge cake has cooled slightly, remove it from the pan.

2 Run a knife around the edges of the pan to gently loosen the sides.

3 Invert the pan and place it over a wire rack.

4 Gently shake the pan to remove cake.

1 Remove the waxed paper.

2 Sprinkle a few drops of water on the top of the waxed paper.

3 Peel the paper off gently and discard.

4 If the sponge cake is not going to be served on the same day, do not remove the paper until the day of serving.

Cutting and Frosting the Cake

1 Place the cooled cake bottom side up on a sheet of parchment or waxed paper.

2 Insert a sharp knife about ¼ to ½ inch deep into the cake to mark where the layers should be cut.

1 Use a piece of heavy thread or fishing line to cut the cake into layers.

2 Place the thread around the cake fitting it into the pre-cut notches.

3 Cross the ends of the thread over and pull firmly. The cross-cut sawing movement of the thread cuts the cake into smooth, even layers.

1 To separate the layers, use a piece of parchment or heavy-duty waxed paper.

2 Gently push the front edge of the paper downward between the layers, holding it as stiffly and as horizontally as possible to keep the cake from breaking.

3 Slide the paper between the layers while holding the upper layer of the cake in place with your index finger.

1 When the paper is completely under the layer, lift it up gently, taking care to hold the paper firmly in a horizontal position.

2 Set the layer aside on the paper.

3 Repeat the process to remove the next layer, if needed.

1 If you prefer to cut the cake with a knife, use one that is sharp and has a serrated blade. The blade should be longer than the diameter of the cake.

2 Again, use pre-cut notches as a guide for cutting the cake.

3 Or, toothpicks can be placed around the edges to guide the cutting.

4 Remove the layer using parchment paper as shown above.

1 Fill the cake with jam or frosting as indicated in the recipe.

2 Use a small metal or rubber spatula or a palette-type knife to spread the filling evenly.

3 Spread the filling to the edges of the layer, but not over the sides.

1 Hold the second layer over the frosted layer, using the paper as a guide.

2 Gently slide the layer off the paper onto the frosted layer.

3 Align the edges of the two layers to prevent them from slipping or becoming lopsided.

1 Spread the top layer with frosting as indicated in the recipe.

2 Spread the frosting gently over the layer with the spatula so that the spatula will not pick up and spread any loose crumbs.

3 Repeat the process if there is a third layer.

1 Smooth the frosting on the top layer.

2 Frost the sides smoothly.

3 If the knife or spatula becomes sticky and will not spread the frosting easily, dip the knife or spatula in warm water and smooth over the rough edges.

1 Sprinkle the sides of the cake with grated chocolate, flaked almonds, chopped walnuts or pecans, or ground hazelnuts.

2 Hold the ingredients very close to the sides of the cake.

3 Press them gently onto the cake while the icing is still soft with a piece of stiff paper or a large rubber scraper.

1 If desired, the cake can be divided into sections before serving or decorating.

2 Use a wooden or metal cake divider.

3 Gently place the divider on top of the cake pressing down only enough to make a slight marking.

1 Use a #32 tube; fill a pastry bag with whipped cream, whipped topping, or buttercream.

2 Hold the bag vertically with your right hand; guide the tube with thumb and index finger of your left hand.

3 Pipe question marks close together along the top edge of the cake, placing one in each section.

4 Cover the tail of the last question mark with the first curve of the next.

5 Pipe a ring of circles in the center.

1 Sprinkle the sides of the cake with grated chocolate.

2 Fill a pastry bag with buttercream; use a #32 pastry tube.

3 Pipe a ring of rosettes around the jelly center; pipe an appropriate number on the jelly.

4 Pipe shells with an up and down movement along the edge of the top, placing one to the right, then one to the left as illustrated.

1 Sprinkle the sides of the cake with blanched, ground roasted hazelnuts while the icing is still soft.

2 Fill a pastry bag with buttercream; use a #32 tube.

3 Pipe elongated shells in a ring in the center of the cake, bringing the points of the shells toward the center.

4 Place hazelnuts between each shell.

5 Pipe elongated shells as an edge border, again bringing the points toward the center.

1 Sprinkle the sides of the cake with grated chocolate while the icing is still soft.

2 Fill a pastry bag with buttercream; use a #32 tube.

3 Form large stars at wide intervals around the top edge of the cake.

4 From each star, form consecutively smaller stars by reducing pressure, finishing with a ring of small stars.

5 Fill the area in the middle with grated chocolate. Garnish the cake with decorative chocolate leaves.

1 Sprinkle the sides of the cake with grated chocolate while icing is still soft.

2 Use any large star tube; fill a pastry bag with buttercream.

3 Pipe simple straight lines onto the cake in a trellis pattern.

4 Finish the top edge of the cake by piping little rosettes closely together.

1 Sprinkle the sides of the cake with blanched, roasted, sliced almonds.

2 Use a #30 or #32 tube; fill a pastry bag with buttercream.

3 Pipe loops close together, starting from the center and making them bigger as they move out toward the edge.

4 Pipe a rosette in the center.

5 Decorate with a candied cherry in the large end of each cone.

1 Sprinkle the sides of the cake with finely chopped pistachios.

2 Use a #32 tube; fill a pastry bag with whipped cream or whipped topping.

3 Pipe question marks around the top edge, ending with a twisted rosette.

4 Pipe a ring in front of each question mark.

1 Sprinkle the sides of the cake with grated or finely chopped flaked coconut.

2 Use a #8 tube; fill a pastry bag with whipped cream or whipped topping.

3 Move tube up and down, using pressure to form the high part of the pattern and releasing it to finish the pattern.

4 Form the middle ring on the top of the cake by piping slanted loops close together.

5 Pipe out a circle of twisted tufts to form the center ring.

1 Spread top of cake with a fruit glaze, reserving a small amount.

2 Use a large star tube; fill a pastry bag with whipped cream.

3 Pipe a flower pattern onto the glaze.

4 Place a little glaze in the center of each "bloom."

5 Decorate the sides of the cake with elongated stars.

1 Tint marzipan paste a light green.

2 Brush a very thin coat of piping gel on the top and sides of the cake.

3 Divide marzipan in half; roll out ½ the same size as the cake; place on top of the cake.

4 Roll second ½ of the marzipan into a long strip; press onto sides.

5 Spread cake with a thin layer of icing tinted light green. Decorate with small Easter eggs.

6 Finish the cake using a #3 tube and white icing.

Covering a Cake with Glaze

1 Place cake on a flat baking sheet.

2 Prepare the glaze as directed in the recipe.

3 If desired, the cake can first be spread with melted jam to prevent the glaze from seeping into the cake.

4 Warm jam in a small saucepan and spread thinly and evenly over the cake.

5 Pour the glaze over the center of the cake.

1 Using a large knife or spatula, quickly spread the glaze over the top and sides of the cake.

2 Hold the knife at a slight angle and press lightly while smoothing the glaze.

3 Spread the glaze in the same direction across the top to prevent crumbs from being picked up and spread by the knife.

4 Spread the glaze evenly up and down the sides of the cake by holding the knife at an angle and spreading smoothly.

1 Transfer the cake to a serving plate as quickly as possible.

2 Loosen the cake from the baking sheet by sliding a large spatula or knife under it.

3 Tilt the baking sheet slightly over the serving plate.

4 Guide the cake onto the serving plate with the knife.

5 Clean up any drips or spills with a damp cloth or paper towel.

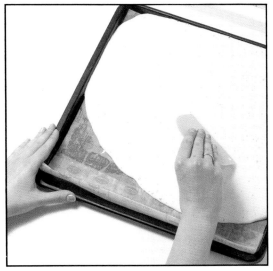

Making a Jelly Roll

1 Grease the pan in about 3 places with butter *or* margarine. **Do not** grease the sides of the pan.

2 Cut waxed paper to fit the jelly-roll pan.

3 Press down firmly and smooth out any wrinkles.

4 Spread the dough about ½ inch thick into the prepared pan using a rubber spatula to spread it evenly.

1 After baking, loosen the cake from the sides of the pan with a knife.

2 With the help of the paper pleat, gently lift out the cake and turn it onto a dish towel that has been sprinkled generously with sugar.

3 Or invert the pan onto the dish towel and shake gently to loosen the cake.

1 Sprinkle the waxed paper with cold water or brush cold water lightly on the paper.

2 Carefully peel the waxed paper off the cake, using a knife to gently scrape off any bits of cake that stick.

3 Discard the paper and smooth top of cake.

4 Gently pat any torn spots in cake back into place.

1 Spoon jelly or jam onto the cake immediately in several places.

2 Use a rubber spatula to spread the jelly evenly over the entire surface, being careful not to tear cake.

1 Quickly, using the towel as a guide, roll up the cake beginning on a long side. As the sponge cake starts to cool, the cake will begin to break as it is rolled up, so it is essential to roll the cake while it is still warm.

2 Leave the cake wrapped in the towel until it is cool. This will help in maintaining the jelly-roll shape.

Basic Sponge Cake

5 eggs
¾ cup sugar
1 teaspoon vanilla
¾ cup flour
2 tablespoons cornstarch
1 teaspoon baking powder

Preheat oven to 400°. Grease and line the bottoms of two 8-inch round cake pans with waxed paper or use a lined 9-inch springform pan.

Beat eggs in a large bowl until light and fluffy. Sprinkle sugar and vanilla over eggs; continue beating for 2 minutes. Sift flour, cornstarch, and baking powder together; sprinkle ½ the mixture over batter. Fold in with rubber spatula. Repeat with remaining flour mixture.

Use a rubber spatula to spread batter evenly in pans. Bake immediately on center rack of oven for 15 to 20 minutes or until cake is golden and springs back when lightly touched.

Invert cake onto wire rack and cool for 5 to 10 minutes; remove pan. Set aside to cool. Cut into 2 layers if using springform pan. Fill, frost, and decorate as desired. Use the guidelines on pages 74-79 for ideas.

Makes 8 to 10 servings

Buche de Noel

5 eggs
¾ cup sugar
1 teaspoon vanilla
¾ cup flour
½ cup cocoa
1 teaspoon baking powder
  Custard Filling
  Cocoa
  Chocolate Buttercream
  Candied cherries,
  optional
  Holly leaves, optional

Preheat oven to 400°. Grease and line a 10 x 15-inch jelly-roll pan with waxed paper.

Beat eggs in a large bowl until light and fluffy. Sprinkle sugar and vanilla over eggs; continue beating for 2 minutes. Sift flour, ½ cup cocoa, and baking powder together. Sprinkle ½ the flour mixture over batter; fold in with rubber spatula. Repeat with remaining flour mixture.

Use a rubber spatula to spread batter evenly in pan. Bake immediately on center rack in oven for 10 to 15 minutes or until cake springs back when lightly touched. While cake is baking, prepare Custard Filling.

Place dish towel on work counter; sprinkle with cocoa. Invert cake onto towel; remove and discard paper. Carefully and quickly, using the towel as a guide, roll up cake, jelly-roll style, beginning on a long side. Leave wrapped in towel to cool. While cake is cooling, prepare Chocolate Buttercream.

Unroll sponge cake and spread with Custard Filling. Reroll the cake, again using the towel as a guide. Cut a 2-inch slice from each end of the cake. Place cake on platter. Place the cut slices on opposite sides of the cake to form "stumps." Use a small amount of Chocolate Buttercream to hold slices in place.

Spread Chocolate Buttercream over cake. Spread the reserved ¼ cup plain buttercream on the four cut edges. Pull a fork over the entire length of the cake to simulate bark. Garnish with candied cherries and holly leaves if desired.

Makes 8 servings

Custard Filling

5 egg yolks
1 cup sugar
½ cup flour
2 cups milk, scalded and cooled
1 tablespoon butter *or* margarine
1 teaspoon vanilla
1 cup whipping cream, chilled

Beat egg yolks in a large bowl until light and fluffy. Sprinkle with sugar; continue beating until sugar has dissolved. Blend in flour. Stir in milk in a slow, steady stream until well mixed.

Pour mixture into a saucepan over medium heat. Bring to a boil, stirring constantly. Reduce heat to simmer; continue to stir for 2 to 3 minutes. Remove from heat. Stir in butter and vanilla; set aside until cooled.

Beat whipping cream until stiff peaks form. Fold into cooled custard.

Chocolate Buttercream

⅓ cup sugar
¼ cup water
3 egg yolks
½ cup butter *or* margarine at room temperature
3 ounces semi-sweet chocolate, melted and cooled
2 ounces unsweetened chocolate, melted and cooled

Combine sugar and water in a small saucepan. Bring mixture to a boil; continue cooking until mixture reaches 236° (soft-ball stage) on a candy thermometer. Remove from heat.

Beat egg yolks in a bowl until light and fluffy; beat in 2 tablespoons of the hot sugar syrup. Pour remaining sugar syrup in a slow, steady stream into the egg yolk mixture, beating constantly until thickened.

Add butter, a little at a time, beating until smooth. Remove ¼ cup of the buttercream and set aside. Add the melted chocolates to the remaining buttercream; beat until smooth.

Truffle Gateau

5 eggs
¾ cup sugar
1 teaspoon vanilla
¾ cup flour
4 tablespoons cornstarch
3 tablespoons cocoa
1 tablespoon baking
   powder
   Chocolate Buttercream
   Chocolate Glaze
1 cup chocolate cookie
   crumbs, divided

Preheat oven to 400°. Grease and line a 9-inch spring-form pan with waxed paper.

Beat eggs in a large bowl until light and fluffy. Sprinkle sugar and vanilla over eggs; continue beating for 2 minutes. Sift flour, cornstarch, cocoa, and baking powder together; sprinkle ½ the flour mixture over batter. Fold in with rubber spatula. Repeat with remaining flour mixture.

Use a rubber spatula to spread batter evenly in prepared pan. Bake immediately for 20 to 30 minutes or until cake springs back when lightly touched. Invert cake onto wire rack and cool for 5 to 10 minutes; remove sides and discard waxed paper. Set aside to cool. Prepare Chocolate Buttercream and Chocolate Glaze while cake is cooling.

Cut the cake into 3 equal layers. Place bottom layer on serving platter and cover with ¼ the Chocolate Buttercream. Place second layer on top and frost with ¼ the buttercream. Top with remaining cake layer. Frost top and sides with remaining buttercream.

Drizzle Chocolate Glaze over the cake. Sprinkle the sides and a ½-inch wide edge around the top of the cake with ½ the cookie crumbs.

Shape truffle balls from the reserved, chilled buttercream. Roll balls in remaining chocolate cookie crumbs. Place truffles around the edge of the cake.

Makes 8 servings

Chocolate Buttercream

¾ cup butter *or* margarine
3 cups confectioners' sugar
1 cup cocoa
1 egg
3 tablespoons dark rum
2 tablespoons milk
1 teaspoon vanilla

Cream butter in a large bowl until light and fluffy. Add sugar and cocoa a little at a time, beating until well blended. Gradually stir in egg and rum. Remove 8 heaping tablespoons of mixture; chill and reserve for garnish. Blend in milk and vanilla.

Chocolate Glaze

6 **ounces semi-sweet chocolate**
2 **tablespoons butter** *or* **margarine**

Melt chocolate and butter in the top of a double boiler over simmering water. Stir until well blended. Cool for 5 minutes.

Mocha Cream Gateau

6 **eggs**
½ **cup sugar**
1 **teaspoon vanilla**
¾ **cup flour**
2 **tablespoons cornstarch**
1 **teaspoon baking powder**
  Mocha Cream
  Chocolate sprinkles

Preheat oven to 400°. Grease and line a 9-inch spring-form pan with waxed paper.

Beat eggs in a large bowl until light and fluffy. Sprinkle sugar and vanilla over eggs; continue beating for 2 minutes. Sift the flour, cornstarch, and baking powder together; sprinkle ½ the flour mixture over batter. Fold in with rubber spatula. Repeat with remaining flour mixture.

Use a rubber spatula to spread batter evenly in prepared pan. Bake immediately for 20 to 30 minutes or until cake is golden and springs back when lightly touched. Invert cake onto wire rack and cool for 5 to 10 minutes; remove sides and discard waxed paper. Set aside to cool. Prepare Mocha Cream while cake is cooling.

Cut the cake into 2 equal layers. Spread bottom layer with ⅓ the Mocha Cream; place remaining cake layer on top. Spread the top and sides evenly with remaining cream. Coat the sides with chocolate sprinkles. Chill until ready to serve. For best results, assemble cake just before serving.

Makes 8 servings

Mocha Cream

3 **tablespoons instant coffee**
3 **cups whipping cream**
¾ **cup confectioners' sugar**
1 **teaspoon vanilla**

Dissolve the instant coffee in 5 tablespoons of whipping cream. Beat remaining cream until soft peaks form. Sprinkle with sugar and vanilla; continue beating until stiff peaks form. Gently stir in the dissolved coffee until well blended.

Chocolate Cream Roll

5 eggs
¾ cup sugar
1 teaspoon vanilla
¾ cup flour
2 tablespoons cornstarch
1 teaspoon baking powder
Chocolate Buttercream
Sugar
Confectioners' sugar

Preheat oven to 400°. Grease and line the bottom of a 10 x 15-inch jelly-roll pan with waxed paper.

Beat eggs in a large bowl until light and fluffy. Sprinkle sugar and vanilla over eggs; continue beating for 2 minutes. Sift flour, cornstarch, and baking powder together. Sprinkle ½ the flour mixture over batter; fold in with rubber spatula. Repeat with remaining flour mixture.

Use a rubber spatula to spread batter evenly in pan. Bake immediately on center rack in oven for 10 to 15 minutes or until cake is golden and springs back when lightly touched. While cake is baking, prepare Chocolate Buttercream.

Place a dish towel on the work counter; sprinkle with sugar. Invert cake onto towel. Remove and discard paper. Carefully and quickly, using the towel as a guide, roll up cake, jelly-roll style, beginning on a long side. Leave wrapped in towel to cool.

Unroll sponge cake. Spread Chocolate Buttercream evenly over cake. Reroll cake, again using towel as a guide. Sprinkle with confectioners' sugar. Cut into ½-inch thick slices before serving.

Makes 8 to 10 servings

Chocolate Buttercream

6 ounces semi-sweet
    chocolate
4 egg yolks
1 cup confectioners' sugar
1⅛ cups butter *or* margarine,
    chilled
3 egg whites
¼ cup sugar

Melt chocolate in top of double boiler over simmering water. Remove from heat; cool for 5 minutes. Combine egg yolks and confectioners' sugar in a small saucepan. Place pan in a larger pan of simmering water or use a double boiler. Beat egg yolks until thick. Remove from heat; cool for 5 to 10 minutes, stirring occasionally. Beat in a small amount of butter at a time; continue beating until all the butter is well blended. Fold in melted chocolate; set aside.

Beat egg whites until soft peaks form. Sprinkle with sugar; continue beating until stiff peaks form. Fold egg whites into chocolate mixture.

Winecream Squares

5 eggs
¾ cup sugar
1 teaspoon vanilla
¾ cup flour
2 tablespoons cornstarch
1 teaspoon baking powder
 Winecream Topping
 Sugar
2 cups fruit, rinsed and
 drained (raspberries, red
 currants, *or* blackberries)
 Currant Glaze

Preheat oven to 400°. Grease and line the bottom of a 10 x 15-inch jelly-roll pan with waxed paper.

Beat eggs in a large bowl until light and fluffy. Sprinkle sugar and vanilla over eggs; continue beating for 2 minutes. Sift flour, cornstarch, and baking powder together; sprinkle ½ the flour mixture over batter. Fold in with rubber spatula; repeat with remaining flour mixture.

Use a rubber spatula to spread batter evenly in prepared pan. Bake immediately on center rack in oven for 10 to 15 minutes or until cake is golden and springs back when lightly touched. Prepare Winecream Topping while cake is baking.

Place a dish towel on work counter; sprinkle generously with sugar. Invert sponge cake onto towel. Remove and discard paper. Invert cake onto large serving platter.

Spread cake with Winecream Topping; arrange fruit over topping. Chill while preparing Currant Glaze. Spread glaze over fruit. Chill until glaze sets. Cut cake into 2-inch squares. Chill until ready to serve.

Makes approximately 36 squares

Winecream Topping

2 packets unflavored
 gelatin
6 tablespoons cold water
1 cup red wine
½ cup water
½ cup sugar
1 teaspoon lemon juice
2 cups whipped cream,
 chilled

Soften gelatin in 6 tablespoons cold water for 5 minutes. Heat wine, ½ cup water, sugar, and lemon juice in small saucepan over medium heat. Stir in gelatin and heat until dissolved, about 3 minutes, stirring constantly. Set aside to cool.

Whip cream until stiff peaks form. Fold in gelatin mixture. Chill until partially set.

Currant Glaze

1 cup currant jelly
5 tablespoons water

Heat jelly and water in small saucepan over medium heat, stirring until it begins to boil. Remove from heat.

Cherry Bombe

5 eggs
¾ cup sugar
1 teaspoon vanilla
¾ cup flour
2 tablespoons cornstarch
1 teaspoon baking powder
  Sugar
1 16-ounce jar cherry jelly
  Cream Filling

Preheat oven to 400°. Grease and line the bottom of a 10 x 15-inch jelly-roll pan with waxed paper.

Beat eggs in a large bowl until light and fluffy. Sprinkle sugar and vanilla over eggs; continue beating for 2 minutes. Sift flour, cornstarch, and baking powder together; sprinkle ½ the mixture over batter. Fold in with rubber spatula. Repeat with remaining flour mixture.

Use a rubber spatula to spread batter evenly in prepared pan. Bake immediately on center rack in oven for 10 to 15 minutes or until cake is golden and springs back when lightly touched. Prepare Cream Filling while cake is baking.

Place a dish towel on work counter; sprinkle with sugar. Invert sponge cake onto towel. Remove and discard paper. Carefully and quickly, using the towel as a guide, roll up the cake, jelly-roll style, beginning on a long side. Leave wrapped in towel and set aside to cool.

Unroll cake and spread with jelly; reroll, again using towel as a guide. Cut into ¼ to ½-inch thick slices. Line a smooth, rounded bowl with the cake slices. Set aside remaining slices. Spoon Cream Filling into cake-lined bowl. Cover with remaining cake slices. Chill for 4 to 5 hours or until firm. To serve, invert mold onto a serving platter. Cut into wedges.

Makes 8 servings

Cream Filling

2 envelopes unflavored
  gelatin
½ cup cold water
3 egg yolks
1 cup sugar, divided
½ cup dry white wine
3 egg whites
1½ cups whipping cream,
  chilled
1 teaspoon vanilla

Sprinkle gelatin over cold water in a small saucepan. Set aside for 5 minutes to soften; stir. Beat egg yolks until light; stir in ⅔ cup sugar and the wine. Continue beating for 1 minute. Place egg yolk mixture in top of double boiler over simmering water. Stir in gelatin mixture until dissolved and eggs are slightly thickened. Stir often; set aside to cool.

Beat egg whites until soft peaks form. Sprinkle with remaining sugar; continue beating until stiff peaks form. Fold egg whites into cooled egg yolk mixture. Beat cream until stiff peaks form; blend in vanilla. Fold whipped cream into egg mixture. Chill for 15 minutes.

Carrot & Nut Cake

5 eggs, separated
2 egg yolks
1 cup sugar, divided
  Zest of 1 lemon
1 tablespoon lemon juice
½ teaspoon anise flavoring
2 cups ground hazelnuts
2 cups grated carrots
½ cup plus 2
  tablespoons flour
1½ teaspoons baking powder
½ cup ground bread crumbs
  Apricot Glaze
  Lemon Icing
½ cup chopped hazelnuts

Preheat oven to 375°. Grease and line a 9-inch spring-form pan with waxed paper.

Beat all of the egg yolks and half of the sugar in a large bowl until light and fluffy. Blend in zest, lemon juice, and anise flavoring. Fold in nuts and carrots. Sift flour and baking powder together; fold into batter with rubber spatula. Blend in bread crumbs.

Beat egg whites in a large bowl until soft peaks form. Sprinkle with remaining sugar; continue beating until stiff peaks form. Fold egg whites into batter.

Use a rubber spatula to spread batter evenly in prepared pan. Bake immediately for 30 to 50 minutes or until cake is golden and springs back when lightly touched. Invert pan onto wire rack and cool for 5 to 10 minutes. Remove sides and discard waxed paper. Set aside.

Prepare Apricot Glaze. Spread glaze over cake; set aside for 15 minutes.

Prepare Lemon Icing. Spread over top and sides of cake. Sprinkle cake with hazelnuts.

Makes 8 to 10 servings

Apricot Glaze

1 cup apricot jam
4 tablespoons water

Combine apricot jam and water in small saucepan. Heat until mixture begins to boil, stirring frequently. Remove from heat.

Lemon Icing

¾ cup butter *or* margarine at
  room temperature
3½ to 4 cups confectioners'
  sugar
2 to 3 tablespoons lemon
  juice
2 to 3 tablespoons water

Cream butter in bowl until smooth and fluffy. Gradually beat in sugar, a little at a time, alternating with juice and water until well blended.

Strawberry Gateau

5 eggs
¾ cup sugar
2 teaspoons vanilla, divided
¾ cup flour
2 tablespoons cornstarch
1 teaspoon baking powder
  Custard Filling
2 cups sliced strawberries *or*
  raspberries
2 cups whipping cream,
  chilled
½ cup confectioners' sugar

Preheat oven to 400°. Grease and line a 9-inch spring-form pan with waxed paper.

Beat eggs in a large bowl until light and fluffy. Sprinkle sugar and 1 teaspoon vanilla over eggs; continue beating for 2 minutes. Sift flour, cornstarch, and baking powder together. Sprinkle ½ the flour mixture over batter; fold in with rubber spatula. Repeat with remaining flour mixture.

Use a rubber spatula to spread batter evenly in pan. Bake immediately for 20 to 30 minutes or until cake is golden and springs back when lightly touched. Prepare Custard Filling while cake is baking.

Invert cake onto wire rack and cool for 5 to 10 minutes; remove sides and discard paper. Set aside to cool.

Cut cake into 2 equal layers. Place bottom layer on serving platter; spread with ½ the custard. Cover with ½ the berries. Cover berries with remaining custard.

Beat whipping cream until stiff peaks form. Stir in remaining berries, confectioners' sugar, and remaining vanilla. Frost sides and top of cake with sweetened whipped cream. Chill until ready to serve. For best results, assemble cake just before serving.

Makes 8 servings

Custard Filling

5 egg yolks
1 cup sugar, divided
½ cup flour
2 cups milk, scalded and
  cooled
1 tablespoon butter *or*
  margarine
1 teaspoon vanilla
3 egg whites

Beat egg yolks in a large bowl until light and fluffy. Sprinkle with ½ cup sugar; continue beating until sugar has dissolved. Blend in flour; stir in milk in a slow, steady stream.

Pour mixture into a saucepan over medium heat. Bring to a boil, stirring constantly. Reduce heat to simmer; continue to stir for 2 to 3 minutes. Remove from heat. Stir in butter and vanilla; set aside until cooled.

Beat egg whites until soft peaks form; sprinkle with remaining sugar. Continue beating until stiff peaks form. Fold egg whites into cooled custard.

Cherry Gateau

Meringue Bases
- 6 eggs
- ½ cup sugar
- 1 teaspoon vanilla
- ¾ cup flour
- 2 tablespoons cornstarch
- 1 teaspoon baking powder
  Buttercream
- 3 tablespoons water
- 3 tablespoons sugar
- 3 tablespoons Kirsch
- ¼ cup toasted almonds

Prepare Meringue Bases.

Preheat oven to 400°. Grease and line the bottom of a 9-inch springform pan with waxed paper.

Beat eggs in a large bowl until light and fluffy. Sprinkle sugar and vanilla over eggs; continue to beat for 2 minutes. Sift flour, cornstarch, and baking powder together. Sprinkle ½ the flour mixture over batter; fold in with rubber spatula. Repeat with remaining flour mixture.

Use a rubber spatula to spread batter evenly in prepared pan. Bake immediately on center rack in oven for 25 to 30 minutes or until cake is golden and springs back when lightly touched. Prepare Buttercream while cake is baking.

Invert cake onto wire rack to cool for 5 to 10 minutes; remove sides and discard paper. Set aside on wire rack to cool. Cut cake into two layers.

Combine water and sugar in small saucepan. Bring to a boil over medium heat. Heat for 5 minutes, stirring often. Stir in Kirsch. Set aside to cool.

Spread 1 of the Meringue Bases with ¼ the Buttercream and place one layer of sponge cake over it. Sprinkle sponge cake with cooled Kirsch syrup and then spread cake with ¼ the remaining buttercream. Place the remaining Meringue Base on top of buttercream; spread with ¼ the remaining buttercream. Place remaining cake layer on top; spread top and sides with remaining buttercream. Press almonds onto the sides of the gateau.

Note: The cake is easier to cut if it is filled one day before it is to be served.

Makes 8 servings

Meringue Bases

4 egg whites
¾ cup sugar
¾ cup ground almonds

Preheat oven to 250°. Line two 9-inch springform pans with waxed paper.

Beat egg whites in a large bowl until soft peaks form. Sprinkle with sugar, a little at a time. Continue beating until stiff but not dry peaks form. Carefully fold in ground almonds.

Divide meringue between the 2 pans and smooth with rubber spatula. Bake for 1 hour. Turn heat off; leave meringues in oven with door closed until they are cool and have become crisp and dry. Remove meringues from pans. Carefully remove and discard paper.

Buttercream

4 egg yolks
1 cup confectioners' sugar
½ cup milk, scalded and cooled
1 cup butter *or* margarine, chilled and cut into small pieces
1 tablespoon Kirsch
1 teaspoon raspberry flavoring

Combine egg yolks and sugar in a medium saucepan. Beat with an electric mixer or whisk until light and slightly thickened. Slowly stir in milk until blended. Place pan in top of double boiler over simmering water. Cook over low heat, stirring constantly until mixture thickens and coats a spoon.

Remove from heat and chill for 20 minutes. Transfer mixture to a large bowl. Beat in butter, a few pieces at a time, until well blended. Stir in Kirsch and raspberry flavoring.

Apricot Cream Gateau

1½ cups flour
2 tablespoons sugar
1 teaspoon vanilla
3 tablespoons butter *or*
   margarine, chilled and cut
   into small pieces
3 tablespoons vegetable
   shortening
3 to 5 tablespoons ice water
   Sponge Cake
   Apricot Filling
2 cups whipping cream
½ cup confectioners' sugar
3 tablespoons apricot jam
   Apricot halves, optional
½ cup chopped roasted
   almonds

Preheat oven to 425°. Grease and line the bottom of a 9-inch springform pan with waxed paper.

Sift flour into a large bowl. Add sugar, vanilla, butter, and shortening. Using a pastry blender or the dough hook of an electric mixer, combine the ingredients until well blended. Add water by the tablespoonful as needed to make dough hold together. Place dough on a lightly floured board; knead until smooth. Roll dough into a ball; cover with plastic wrap and chill for 20 minutes.

Roll out dough to fit pan or pat dough onto the base of prepared springform pan. Prick dough several times with a fork; replace sides of pan. Bake for 10 to 15 minutes or until golden. Place on wire rack; cool for 5 to 10 minutes.

Remove sides of pan; set crust aside to cool. Prepare Sponge Cake and Apricot Filling while crust is cooling. Place cooled crust on serving plate.

Beat whipping cream until soft peaks form. Sprinkle confectioners' sugar over cream. Beat until stiff peaks form. Stir ½ the whipped cream into the chilled Apricot Filling; set aside. Reserve remaining whipped cream.

Spread apricot jam over crust. Place one layer of sponge cake over base; spread with Apricot Filling. Top with remaining cake layer; press gently into place. Cover top and sides of cake with reserved whipped cream.

Decorate with any remaining filling; garnish with apricot halves, if desired. Sprinkle sides of cake with chopped almonds. Chill until ready to serve.

Makes 8 to 10 servings

Sponge Cake

6 eggs
¾ cup sugar
1 teaspoon vanilla
¾ cup flour
2 tablespoons cornstarch
1 teaspoon baking powder
3 tablespoons butter *or* margarine, melted and cooled

Reduce oven temperature to 375°. Line the bottom of a 9-inch springform pan with waxed paper or use two 9-inch round cake pans.

Beat eggs in a large bowl until light and fluffy. Sprinkle sugar and vanilla over eggs; continue beating for 2 minutes. Sift flour, cornstarch, and baking powder together; sprinkle ½ the flour mixture over batter. Fold in with rubber spatula. Repeat with remaining flour mixture. Fold in cooled butter.

Use a rubber spatula to spread batter evenly in prepared pan. Bake immediately on center rack in oven for 20 to 30 minutes or until cake is golden and springs back when lightly touched.

Invert cake onto wire rack to cool for 5 to 10 minutes; remove pan and discard paper. Set aside to cool. If using springform pan, cut cake into 2 equal layers when cooled.

Apricot Filling

1 1-pound, 13-ounce can apricots
3 tablespoons cornstarch
¼ cup sugar
1 tablespoon lemon juice

Drain apricots; reserve liquid. Purée apricots in blender. Combine reserved liquid and enough water to make 1 cup. Mix 4 tablespoons of apricot liquid with cornstarch and sugar in small bowl; set aside. Bring remaining liquid to a boil over medium heat, stirring often, until mixture begins to thicken. Stir in cornstarch mixture; cook 2 minutes longer, stirring frequently. Remove from heat; stir in apricot purée. Chill for 15 minutes. Stir in lemon juice.

Chocolate Cream Gateau

6 eggs
½ cup sugar
1 teaspoon vanilla
¾ cup flour
2 tablespoons cornstarch
1 teaspoon baking powder
Chocolate Buttercream
Chocolate sprinkles
Shaved chocolate curls

Preheat oven to 400°. Grease and line a 9-inch springform pan with waxed paper.

Beat eggs in a large bowl until light and fluffy. Sprinkle sugar and vanilla over eggs; continue beating for 2 minutes. Sift the flour, cornstarch, and baking powder together; sprinkle ½ the flour mixture over batter. Fold in with rubber spatula. Repeat with remaining flour mixture.

Use a rubber spatula to spread batter evenly into pan. Bake immediately for 20 to 30 minutes or until cake is golden and springs back when lightly touched. Invert cake onto wire rack and cool for 5 to 10 minutes; remove sides and discard paper. Set aside to cool. Prepare Chocolate Buttercream while cake is cooling.

Cut the cake into 3 equal layers. Spread bottom layer with ¼ the Chocolate Buttercream; place second cake layer on top. Spread with ¼ the buttercream. Top with third layer. Spread top and sides evenly with ¼ the buttercream. Coat the sides with chocolate sprinkles. Pipe remaining buttercream in decorative rows across top of cake. Garnish with chocolate curls. Chill until ready to serve. For best results, assemble cake just before serving.

Makes 8 servings

Chocolate Buttercream

¾ cup butter *or* margarine
3 cups confectioners' sugar
1 cup cocoa
1 egg
2 teaspoons vanilla

Cream butter in a large bowl until fluffy. Add sugar and cocoa, a little at a time, beating until well blended. Gradually stir in egg. Blend in vanilla.

Chocolate Cream Gateau, this page

Lemon Roll

5 eggs
¾ cup sugar
1 teaspoon vanilla
¾ cup flour
1 teaspoon baking powder
  Lemon Cream Filling
  Sugar

Preheat oven to 400°. Grease and line a 10 x 15-inch jelly-roll pan with waxed paper.

Beat eggs in a large bowl until light and fluffy. Sprinkle with sugar and vanilla; continue beating for 2 minutes. Sift the flour and baking powder together. Sprinkle ½ the mixture over batter; fold in with rubber spatula. Repeat with remaining flour mixture.

Use a rubber spatula to spread batter evenly in pan. Bake immediately on center rack of oven for 10 to 15 minutes or until cake is golden and springs back when lightly touched. Prepare Lemon Cream Filling while cake is baking.

Place a dish towel on work counter; sprinkle with sugar. Invert cake onto towel; remove and discard paper. Carefully and quickly, using the towel as a guide, roll up cake, jelly-roll style, beginning on a long side. Leave wrapped in towel to cool.

Unroll cooled sponge cake. Spread it with ⅔ of the Lemon Cream Filling. Reroll the cake, again using the towel as a guide. Spread the top of the roll with the remaining filling. Chill until ready to serve.

Makes 8 to 10 servings

Lemon Cream Filling

2 packages unflavored gelatin
6 tablespoons cold water
  Zest of ½ lemon
3 tablespoons sugar
5 tablespoons lemon juice
2 cups whipping cream, chilled
1 cup confectioners' sugar

Soften gelatin in cold water in a small saucepan for 5 minutes. Simmer until dissolved, stirring often. Stir in zest, sugar, and lemon juice; set aside. Whip cream until soft peaks form. Sprinkle with confectioners' sugar; fold in lemon mixture. Continue beating until stiff peaks form.

Strawberry Roll

(Illustrated on pp. 66-67)

6 eggs
¾ cup sugar
1 teaspoon vanilla
¾ cup flour
2 tablespoons cornstarch
1 teaspoon baking powder
　Strawberry Filling
　Sugar
　Chopped pistachio nuts

Preheat oven to 400°. Grease and line the bottom of a 10 x 15-inch jelly-roll pan with waxed paper.

Beat eggs in a large bowl until light and fluffy. Sprinkle sugar and vanilla over eggs; continue beating for 2 minutes. Sift flour, cornstarch, and baking powder together. Sprinkle ½ the flour mixture over batter; fold in with rubber spatula. Repeat with remaining flour mixture.

Use a rubber spatula to spread batter evenly in prepared pan. Bake immediately on center rack of oven for 10 to 15 minutes or until cake is golden and springs back when lightly touched. Prepare Strawberry Filling while cake is baking.

Place a dish towel on work counter; sprinkle generously with sugar. Invert sponge cake onto towel. Remove and discard paper. Carefully and quickly, using the towel as a guide, roll up the cake, jelly-roll style, beginning on a long side. Leave wrapped in towel to cool.

Unroll the sponge cake on a flat surface and spread it evenly with Strawberry Filling. Reroll, again using towel as a guide. Place on serving platter, seam side down. Spread outside of roll with remaining whipped cream. Sprinkle with chopped pistachio nuts. Trim ends. Chill until ready to serve.

Note: Assemble just before serving for best results.

Makes 8 to 10 servings

Strawberry Filling

1 pint strawberries, hulled, washed and drained
2 cups whipping cream, chilled
½ cups confectioners' sugar, sifted
1 teaspoon vanilla

Pat drained berries with paper towels; slice. Rub 4 tablespoons of the berries through a sieve, set aside. Whip cream until soft peaks form. Sprinkle with sugar and vanilla; continue beating until stiff peaks form. Divide whipped cream in half. Stir strawberry pieces and pulp into half the whipped cream. Set remaining whipped cream aside.

Chocolate Cream Torte

6 eggs
½ cup sugar
1 teaspoon vanilla
¾ cup flour
1 teaspoon baking powder
Chocolate Filling

Preheat oven to 400°. Grease and line a 9-inch spring-form pan with waxed paper.

Beat eggs in a large bowl until light and fluffy. Sprinkle with sugar and vanilla; continue beating for 2 minutes. Sift the flour and baking powder together. Sprinkle ½ the mixture over batter; fold in with rubber spatula. Repeat with remaining flour mixture.

Use a rubber spatula to spread batter evenly in pan. Bake immediately on center rack of oven for 25 to 30 minutes or until cake is golden and springs back when lightly touched. Prepare Chocolate Filling while cake is baking.

Cool cake inverted on wire rack for 5 to 10 minutes. Remove sides and discard paper. Set aside to cool.

Cut the cake into 2 equal layers. Place 1 layer on serving plate. Spread the layer with ⅓ of the Chocolate Filling. Top with remaining layer. Spread the top and sides of the cake with remaining filling.

Makes 8 to 10 servings

Chocolate Filling

1½ cups sugar
½ cup water
6 egg yolks
1¾ cups butter *or* margarine
at room temperature
2 ounces semi-sweet
chocolate, melted and
cooled
1 ounce bitter chocolate,
melted and cooled
½ cup cocoa

Combine sugar and water in a small saucepan. Bring mixture to a boil; stir and continue cooking until mixture reaches 240° (soft-ball stage) on a candy thermometer. Remove from heat.

Beat egg yolks in a bowl until light and fluffy; beat in 2 tablespoons of the hot sugar syrup. Pour remaining sugar syrup in a slow, steady stream into the egg yolk mixture, beating constantly until thickened.

Cream butter in a bowl until light and fluffy. Blend in melted chocolates and cocoa. Stir into egg mixture.

Custard Slices

5 eggs
¾ cup sugar
1 teaspoon vanilla
¾ cup flour
3 tablespoons cornstarch
1 teaspoon baking powder
Custard Filling
Sugar
½ cup raspberry jam
Confectioners' sugar

Preheat oven to 400°. Grease and line a 10 x 15-inch jelly-roll pan with waxed paper.

Beat eggs in a large bowl until light and fluffy. Sprinkle sugar and vanilla over eggs; continue beating for 2 minutes. Sift flour, cornstarch, and baking powder together. Sprinkle ½ the flour mixture over batter; fold in with rubber spatula. Repeat with remaining flour mixture.

Use a rubber spatula to spread batter evenly in pan. Bake immediately on center rack of oven for 10 to 15 minutes or until cake is golden and springs back when lightly touched. While cake is baking, prepare Custard Filling.

Place a dish towel on work counter; sprinkle with sugar. Invert cake onto towel. Remove and discard paper; set aside to cool. Cut cake in half.

Place one half on serving platter. Spread with raspberry jam. Cover jam with Custard Filling. Top gently with remaining cake half. Sprinkle with confectioners' sugar. Cut into 4 x 2-inch slices.

Makes 8 to 10 servings

Custard Filling

5 egg yolks
1 cup sugar
½ cup flour
2 cups milk, scalded and cooled
1 tablespoon butter *or* margarine
1 teaspoon vanilla
1 cup whipping cream, chilled

Beat egg yolks in a large bowl until light and fluffy. Sprinkle with sugar; continue beating until sugar has dissolved. Blend in flour. Stir in milk in a slow, steady stream until well mixed.

Pour mixture into a saucepan over medium heat. Bring to a boil, stirring constantly. Reduce heat to simmer; continue to stir for 2 to 3 minutes. Remove from heat. Stir in butter and vanilla; set aside until cooled.

Beat whipping cream until stiff peaks form. Fold into cooled custard.

Black Forest Gateau

1 cup cake flour
3 tablespoons cocoa
¼ teaspoon baking powder
2 tablespoons sugar
¼ teaspoon salt
3 tablespoons butter *or*
    margarine at room
    temperature
3 tablespoons vegetable
    shortening
3 to 5 tablespoons ice water
    Chocolate Cake
1 1-pound, 13-ounce can
    dark pitted cherries,
    drained
¼ cup sugar
4 to 5 tablespoons Kirsch
    Whipped Cream Filling
    Shaved chocolate curls

Preheat oven to 425°. Grease and line a 9-inch spring-form pan with waxed paper.

Combine first 7 ingredients in large bowl. Use a pastry blender or the dough hook of an electric mixer to blend ingredients. Add water by the tablespoonful only until dough holds together.

Place dough on a lightly floured board; knead until smooth. Roll dough into a ball; cover with plastic wrap and chill for 20 minutes. Roll out dough to fit pan or pat dough into bottom of prepared pan. Replace sides of pan. Prick dough several times with a fork.

Bake for 10 to 15 minutes or until lightly browned. Remove from oven; cool for 5 to 10 minutes. Remove crust from pan; place on wire rack to cool. Prepare Chocolate Cake while crust is cooling.

Mix cherries with sugar and Kirsch in small bowl; set aside. Prepare Whipped Cream Filling.

Place cooled crust on serving platter. Spread with ½ the cherry mixture and top cherries with ¼ the whipped cream. Place one cake layer over the whipped cream and press gently into place. Spread with remaining cherry mixture. Cover cherries with ¼ the whipped cream. Place remaining cake layer over whipped cream. Spread the top and sides of the cake with remaining whipped cream.

Sprinkle top of cake with chocolate curls. Refrigerate cake until ready to serve. For best results, assemble cake just prior to serving.

Makes 8 servings

Chocolate Cake

6 egg yolks
¼ cup sugar
1 teaspoon vanilla
¾ cup flour
3 tablespoons cocoa
1 teaspoon baking powder

Preheat oven to 400°. Grease and line a 9-inch spring-form pan with waxed paper.

Beat egg yolks in large bowl until light and fluffy. Sprinkle sugar and vanilla over eggs; continue beating for 2 minutes. Sift flour, cocoa, baking powder, and cinnamon together. Sprinkle ½ the mixture over

(continued on next page)

¼ teaspoon ground
   cinnamon
6 egg whites, stiffly beaten
   with ¼ cup sugar

batter; fold in with rubber spatula. Repeat with remaining flour mixture. Fold in beaten egg whites.

Use a rubber spatula to spread batter evenly in pan. Bake immediately for 25 to 30 minutes or until cake springs back when lightly touched. Cool in pan inverted on wire rack for 5 to 10 minutes. Remove sides and discard paper. Set aside to cool. Cut cooled cake into 2 equal layers.

Whipped Cream Filling

3 cups whipping cream,
   chilled
½ cup confectioners' sugar
1 teaspoon vanilla

Whip cream in large bowl until soft peaks form. Sprinkle with sugar and vanilla. Continue beating until stiff peaks form.

Vanilla Ice Cream Roll

5 eggs
¾ cup sugar
1 teaspoon vanilla
¾ cup flour
2 tablespoons orange zest
   Sugar
   Butterscotch Sauce
½ gallon French vanilla ice
   cream, softened
   Confectioners' sugar

Preheat oven to 400°. Grease and line the bottom of a 10 x 15-inch jelly-roll pan with waxed paper.

Beat eggs in a large bowl until light and fluffy. Sprinkle sugar and vanilla over eggs; continue beating for 2 minutes. Sift the flour over batter; fold in with rubber spatula. Repeat with remaining flour. Stir in orange zest.

Use rubber spatula to spread batter evenly in pan. Bake immediately on center rack in oven for 10 to 15 minutes or until cake is golden and springs back when lightly touched.

Place a dish towel on work counter; sprinkle with sugar. Invert sponge cake onto towel. Remove and discard paper. Carefully and quickly, using the towel as a guide, roll up the cake, jelly-roll style, beginning on a long side. Leave wrapped in towel and set aside to cool.

Prepare Butterscotch Sauce; keep warm until ready to serve. Unroll cake; spread with softened ice cream. Reroll cake; freeze until 5 minutes before serving. Cut into ¾-inch thick slices. Serve with warm Butterscotch Sauce. Sprinkle with confectioners' sugar.

Makes 8 to 10 servings

Butterscotch Sauce

1 egg yolk, slightly beaten
½ cup butter *or* margarine
¾ cup firmly packed light
   brown sugar
¼ cup light corn syrup

Combine all ingredients in top of double boiler over simmering water. Stir over medium heat until sauce thickens.

Swiss Roll

5 eggs
¾ cup sugar
1 teaspoon vanilla
¾ cup flour
2 tablespoons cornstarch
1 teaspoon baking powder
   Sugar
2 cups raspberry jam
   Confectioners' sugar,
   sifted

Preheat oven to 400°. Grease and line a 10 x 15-inch jelly-roll pan with waxed paper.

Beat eggs in a large bowl until light and fluffy. Sprinkle sugar and vanilla over eggs; continue beating for 2 minutes. Sift flour, cornstarch, and baking powder together. Sprinkle ½ the mixture over batter; fold in with rubber spatula. Repeat with remaining flour mixture.

Use a rubber spatula to spread batter evenly in prepared pan. Bake immediately on center rack for 10 to 15 minutes or until cake is golden and springs back when lightly touched.

While cake is baking, place a dish towel on counter; sprinkle generously with sugar. Invert sponge cake onto towel. Remove and discard paper. Carefully and quickly, using the towel as a guide, roll up cake, jelly-roll style, beginning on a long side. Leave cake wrapped in towel and set aside to cool.

Unroll cake on flat surface. Spread it evenly with raspberry jam. Reroll, again using towel as a guide. Trim ends. Sprinkle top of roll with confectioners' sugar.

Makes 8 to 10 servings

Marzipan Gateau

5 eggs
¾ cup sugar
1 teaspoon vanilla
¾ cup flour
3 tablespoons cornstarch
1 teaspoon baking powder
  Mocha Cream Filling
2 cups almond paste
  (available at gourmet
  stores)
1 cup confectioners' sugar
4 ounces semi-sweet
  chocolate
2 tablespoons butter *or*
  margarine

Preheat oven to 400°. Grease and line a 9-inch spring-form pan with waxed paper.

Beat eggs in a large bowl until light and fluffy. Sprinkle sugar and vanilla over eggs; continue beating for 2 minutes. Sift flour, cornstarch, and baking powder together. Sprinkle ½ the flour mixture over batter; fold in with rubber spatula. Repeat with remaining flour mixture.

Use a rubber spatula to spread batter evenly in pan. Bake immediately on center rack of oven for 25 to 30 minutes or until cake is golden and springs back when lightly touched. Prepare Mocha Cream Filling while cake is baking.

Invert cake onto wire rack for 5 to 10 minutes; remove sides and discard paper. Set aside to cool.

Cut cake into 3 equal layers. Place bottom layer on serving plate; spread with ½ the Mocha Cream Filling. Place second layer on top of cream; spread with remaining filling. Place third layer on top; set aside.

Knead almond paste and confectioners' sugar together to make marzipan. Roll out marzipan thinly. Cut out a circle the same size as the cake; reroll remaining marzipan into a thin strip long enough to encircle cake. Place the circle on top of cake; trim the strip to fit around the sides of the cake. Press marzipan onto top and sides of cake.

Melt chocolate and butter in top of double boiler over simmering water. Stir until well blended; cool for 5 minutes. Drizzle chocolate over the top and sides of cake.

Makes 8 servings

Mocha Cream Filling

5 egg yolks
1 cup sugar, divided
½ cup flour
2 cups milk, scalded and
  cooled

Beat egg yolks in a large bowl until light and fluffy. Sprinkle with ½ cup sugar; continue beating until sugar has dissolved. Blend in flour; stir in milk in a slow, steady stream until well mixed.

Pour mixture into a saucepan over medium heat.

1 tablespoon butter *or*
  margarine
2 teaspoons instant coffee
2 tablespoons mocha
  liqueur, optional
3 egg whites

Bring to a boil, stirring constantly. Reduce heat to simmer; continue to stir for 2 to 3 minutes. Remove from heat; stir in butter, coffee, and liqueur. Set aside to cool.

Beat egg whites until soft peaks form. Sprinkle with remaining sugar; continue beating until stiff peaks form. Fold into cooled custard.

Hazelnut Torte

7 eggs, separated
1½ cups sugar, divided
1 teaspoon vanilla
¼ teaspoon salt
3 cups ground hazelnuts
⅓ cup cake flour
2 cups whipping cream,
  chilled
1 cup currant jelly
½ cup whole hazelnuts

Preheat oven to 375°. Grease and line a 9-inch springform pan with waxed paper.

Beat egg yolks in large bowl until light and fluffy. Sprinkle with ¾ cup sugar; continue beating for 2 minutes. Blend in vanilla and salt; set aside.

Beat egg whites until soft peaks form. Sprinkle with ¼ cup sugar; continue beating until stiff peaks form. Fold in ground hazelnuts. Fold beaten egg whites into yolk mixture. Sift flour over batter; fold in with rubber spatula.

Use a rubber spatula to spread batter evenly in pan. Bake immediately for 20 to 25 minutes or until cake is golden and springs back when lightly touched. Invert cake onto wire rack to cool for 5 to 10 minutes; remove sides and discard paper. Set aside to cool.

While cake is cooling, beat cream in a large bowl until soft peaks form. Sprinkle with remaining sugar; continue beating until stiff peaks form.

Cut cake into 3 equal layers. Spread jelly over each layer of cake. Place a cake layer on serving plate; cover with ¼ the whipped cream. Place second layer on top and cover with ¼ the whipped cream. Place remaining cake layer on top. Frost top and sides of cake with remaining whipped cream.

Chill until ready to serve. Garnish with whole hazelnuts. For best results, assemble just before serving time.

Makes 8 servings

Orange Cream Cake

5 eggs
¾ cup sugar
1 teaspoon vanilla
¾ cup flour
¼ cup cocoa
1 teaspoon baking powder
½ cup roasted ground
   almonds
   Orange Cream Filling
2 ounces semi-sweet
   chocolate, melted

Preheat oven to 400°. Grease and line a 9-inch spring-form pan with waxed paper.

Beat eggs in a large bowl until light and fluffy. Sprinkle with sugar and vanilla; continue beating for 2 minutes. Sift the flour, cocoa, and baking powder together. Sprinkle ½ the mixture over batter; fold in with rubber spatula. Repeat with remaining flour mixture. Fold in almonds.

Use a rubber spatula to spread batter evenly in pan. Bake immediately on center rack of oven for 25 to 30 minutes or until cake springs back when lightly touched. Prepare Orange Cream Filling while cake is baking.

Cool cake inverted on wire rack for 5 to 10 minutes. Remove sides and discard paper. Set aside to cool.

Cut cake into 2 equal layers. Line the sides of the springform pan with waxed paper. Place the lined sides around the cake layer on the serving plate; fasten sides securely.

Reserve 1 cup of the Orange Cream Filling; spread remaining filling on the bottom layer of cake. Stir the melted chocolate and the remaining orange juice into the reserved whipped cream. Place second cake layer over the first. Spread whipped cream mixture over top of cake. Chill with pan sides in place for 30 minutes or longer before serving.

Remove pan sides and discard waxed paper. Frost sides of cake with reserved Orange Cream Filling. Keep chilled until ready to serve. For best results, frost sides of cake just before serving.

Makes 8 to 10 servings

Orange Cream Filling

1 package unflavored
   gelatin
4 tablespoons water
   Zest of ½ orange
¾ cup orange juice, divided

Place gelatin and water in small saucepan to soften; set aside for 5 minutes. Stir gelatin and heat until dissolved. Stir in zest, ½ cup orange juice, and sugar. Heat until mixture comes to a boil, stirring often. Set aside to cool.

¼ cup sugar
2 cups whipping cream, chilled

Beat whipping cream in a large bowl until stiff peaks form. Stir ⅔ the whipped cream into the cooled orange juice mixture. Set remaining whipped cream aside.

Orange Gateau

5 eggs
¾ cup sugar
1 teaspoon vanilla
¾ cup flour
3 tablespoons cornstarch
1 teaspoon baking powder
Orange Buttercream
Sugar

Preheat oven to 400°. Grease and line a 10 x 15-inch jelly-roll pan with waxed paper.

Beat eggs in a large bowl until light and fluffy. Sprinkle with sugar and vanilla; continue beating for 2 minutes. Sift flour, cornstarch, and baking powder together. Sprinkle ½ the flour mixture over batter; fold in with rubber spatula. Repeat with remaining flour mixture.

Use a rubber spatula to spread batter evenly in prepared pan. Bake immediately for 15 to 20 minutes or until cake is golden and springs back when lightly touched. Prepare Orange Buttercream while cake is baking.

Place a dish towel on work counter; sprinkle with sugar. Invert cake onto towel to cool. Remove and discard paper.

Cut cooled cake into 3 equal pieces. Spread 1 piece with ¼ the Orange Buttercream. Place second piece atop the first. Spread it with ¼ of the buttercream. Place third piece on top. Spread top and sides of cake thinly and evenly with remaining buttercream.

Makes 8 servings

Orange Buttercream

2 eggs
1½ cups sugar
1½ cups butter *or* margarine
2 tablespoons orange zest
2 tablespoons orange liqueur *or* orange juice

Combine eggs and sugar in a saucepan. Beat over medium-low heat with electric hand mixer or whisk until light and slightly thickened. Place saucepan in the top of a double boiler over simmering water. Heat on low, stirring constantly, until mixture coats a spoon. Chill for 20 minutes. Transfer to a large bowl. Beat in butter, a few pieces at a time until well blended. Stir in zest and orange liqueur.

Mandarin Omelets

2 eggs
½ cup sugar, divided
1 teaspoon vanilla
⅓ cup flour
5 tablespoons cornstarch
⅓ cup butter *or* margarine,
  melted and cooled
  Confectioners' sugar
1 12-ounce can mandarin
  orange segments
2 tablespoons lemon juice
1½ cups whipping cream

Use aluminum foil to prepare 14 baking molds. The molds should be round, 4 inches in diameter, with 2-inch high rims. Grease each mold well.

Preheat oven to 375°. Place a medium bowl inside a large bowl or saucepan partially filled with hot water. Add eggs, ¼ cup of sugar, and vanilla to medium bowl; beat until eggs are foamy. Remove bowl from hot water bath and beat again. Sift flour and cornstarch together. Sprinkle flour mixture over eggs; fold in with rubber spatula. Stir in butter, a little at a time, until well blended.

Divide batter evenly among molds. Bake immediately for 8 to 12 minutes. Loosen omelets from molds; place on wire rack to cool. Dust lightly with confectioners' sugar.

Drain orange segments, reserving juice; set segments aside. Combine reserved juice, lemon juice, and 1 teaspoon sugar in large bowl; blend well. Add whipping cream; beat until soft peaks form. Add remaining sugar; beat until stiff peaks form.

Pipe or spoon whipped cream into omelets; fold omelets over and garnish with orange segments.

Makes 14 servings

Ladyfingers

3 eggs, separated, yolks
  well beaten
½ cup sugar
1 teaspoon vanilla
¾ cup flour
  Confectioners' sugar

Preheat oven to 350°. Grease and lightly flour a 10 x 15-inch jelly-roll pan or ladyfinger pan.

Beat egg whites until soft peaks form. Sprinkle with sugar; continue beating until stiff peaks form. Fold in vanilla and egg yolks. Sift flour over mixture; fold in with rubber spatula.

Fill a pastry bag with mixture; place a ½-inch round tip on pastry bag. Pipe 4 x 1¼-inch strips onto prepared pan. Sift confectioners' sugar over ladyfingers. Bake for 12 to 15 minutes or until lightly golden. Remove from pan; place on wire rack to cool.

Store ladyfingers in an airtight container. For best results, use within 2 to 3 days.

Makes 18 ladyfingers

Nut Cream Gateau

6 eggs
¾ cup sugar
1 teaspoon vanilla
¾ cup flour
3 tablespoons cornstarch
1 teaspoon baking powder
  Hazelnut Filling

Preheat oven to 400°. Grease and line a 9-inch spring-form pan with waxed paper.

Beat eggs in large bowl until light and fluffy. Sprinkle sugar and vanilla over eggs; continue beating for 2 minutes. Sift flour, cornstarch, and baking powder together. Sprinkle ½ the flour mixture over batter; fold in with rubber spatula. Repeat with remaining flour mixture.

Use a rubber spatula to spread batter evenly in pan. Bake immediately on center rack of oven for 20 to 30 minutes or until cake is golden and springs back when lightly touched. Prepare Hazelnut Filling while cake is baking.

Invert cake on wire rack to cool for 5 to 10 minutes; remove sides and discard paper. Set aside to cool.

Cut cooled cake into two equal layers. Spread bottom layer with ⅓ the Hazelnut Filling. Place remaining layer on top and press down gently. Spread top and sides of cake with remaining filling. Sprinkle sides with reserved hazelnuts. Chill until ready to serve. For best results, assemble cake just before serving.

Makes 8 servings

Hazelnut Filling

2 cups whipping cream,
  chilled
¼ cup confectioners' sugar
1 teaspoon vanilla
1½ cup ground hazelnuts,
  divided

Beat whipping cream in a large bowl until soft peaks form. Sprinkle with sugar and vanilla; continue beating until stiff peaks form. Fold in 1¼ cups hazelnuts. Reserve remaining hazelnuts.

Sacher Torte

4 ounces semi-sweet
   chocolate
½ cup butter *or* margarine
6 eggs, separated
1 cup sugar, divided
¾ cup flour
3½ ounces ground almonds
   Chocolate Glaze
1 cup apricot jam, divided

Heat chocolate and butter in double boiler over simmering water, stirring until melted. Set aside to cool.

Preheat oven to 400°. Grease and line a 9-inch springform pan with waxed paper.

Beat egg yolks and ½ the sugar in a large bowl until light and fluffy. Blend in cooled chocolate; set aside. Beat egg whites until soft peaks form. Sprinkle with remaining sugar; continue beating until stiff peaks form. Fold chocolate mixture into egg whites with rubber spatula; blend in flour and ground almonds.

Use a rubber spatula to spread batter evenly in prepared pan. Bake for 30 minutes or until cake is golden and springs back when lightly touched. Prepare Chocolate Glaze while cake is baking. Remove cake from oven and cool in pan for 5 minutes. Invert onto wire rack and cool for 5 to 10 minutes; remove sides and waxed paper. Set aside to cool.

Cut cooled cake into 3 equal layers. Spread the bottom layer with ½ cup of jam. Top with second layer and spread with remaining jam. Place third layer on top and press gently into place. Spread top and sides of cake with Chocolate Glaze. Set aside until chocolate is firm.

Makes 8 servings

Chocolate Glaze

8 ounces semi-sweet
   chocolate
3 tablespoons butter *or*
margarine

Heat chocolate and butter in top of double boiler over simmering water, stirring until well blended.

Rascals

5 eggs, separated
¼ teaspoon salt
¼ teaspoon lemon juice
¾ cup sugar, divided
¼ teaspoon vanilla
½ cup cake flour
½ cup ground toasted
    hazelnuts
    Confectioners' sugar
    Frosting
    Whole hazelnuts

Preheat oven to 350°. Grease and line the bottom of a 10 x 15-inch jelly-roll pan.

Beat egg whites, salt, and lemon juice in a large bowl until soft peaks form. Gradually add 3 tablespoons of sugar and beat until stiff peaks form. Beat egg yolks, remaining sugar, and vanilla in a separate bowl until thick and light-colored. Blend in flour. Gently fold in the egg whites and ground nuts, a little at a time.

Use rubber spatula to spread batter evenly in prepared pan. Bake for about 20 minutes or until cake is golden and springs back when lightly touched. Set aside for 5 minutes. Invert onto a dish towel sprinkled with sugar. Remove pan and peel off paper. Set aside until completely cool. Prepare Frosting.

Cut cake in half. Place one layer on a serving plate. Spread with ¼ the Frosting. Top with second layer. Spread ½ the remaining Frosting evenly over top and sides, reserving remainder for garnish.

Fill a pastry bag fitted with a star tip with the reserved Frosting and pipe rosettes on top of cake. Top each rosette with a hazelnut. Refrigerate until firm. Cut into squares and serve.

Makes approximately 16 servings

Frosting

1½ cups whipping cream
10 ounces semi-sweet
     chocolate
1   ounce unsweetened
     chocolate
2   tablespoons rum

Bring whipping cream to a boil in a saucepan. Reduce heat and stir in chocolates; stir until melted, but *do not* boil. Place pan in a larger container filled with ice cubes, stirring occasionally, until mixture is the consistency of pudding. Remove from ice. Stir in rum; beat until thick and fluffy.

Hidden Treasure Cake

10 ounces semi-sweet chocolate, divided
¼ cup flour plus 2 table-spoons
2 tablespoons unsweetened cocoa
4 eggs, separated
¼ cup sugar
¼ teaspoon lemon juice
Filling
¼ cup apricot jam, melted
¼ cup whipping cream

Preheat oven to 350°. Grease and line the bottom of a 10 x 15-inch jelly-roll pan.

Melt 4½ ounces of the chocolate in a double boiler over simmering water; set aside to cool slightly. Sift flour and cocoa together; set aside. Beat egg yolks and sugar in a large bowl until thick and light-colored. Blend in melted chocolate. Beat egg whites and lemon juice in a separate bowl until stiff peaks form. Alternately fold flour mixture and egg whites into egg yolks. Do not over mix.

Use a rubber spatula to spread batter evenly in prepared pan. Bake for 15 to 20 minutes or until cake springs back when lightly touched. Set aside for 3 to 4 minutes. Turn out onto a dish towel sprinkled with sugar. Peel off paper. Set aside until completely cool. Prepare Filling.

Cut cake in half; trim edges. Place one layer on serving plate; spread with Filling. Top with second layer; press down lightly. Chill until Filling is firm.

Spread top with jam. Combine remaining chocolate and cream in a small saucepan over very low heat, stirring until smooth. Pour over top of cake. Quickly spread with spatula. Chill until firm. Cut into squares.

Makes approximately 16 servings

Filling

3 egg yolks
1 cup confectioners' sugar
¼ cup milk, scalded
1 cup butter at room temperature
2 tablespoons rum
½ tablespoon strong coffee

Beat egg yolks and sugar until thick and light-colored. Gradually stir in hot milk; return to saucepan. Cook over low heat, stirring constantly, until mixture coats a spoon. Remove from heat. Place in a large container filled with ice water. Stir until lukewarm. Beat in butter a little at a time. Blend in rum and coffee.

Tarts, Pies, and Cookies

Tarts, Pies, and Cookies

A versatile dough that can be made into pies, cakes, strudels, tarts, flans, and cookies is the kneaded dough.

Kneaded dough is somewhat of a cross between cake and pastry dough. Because of the butter used to make the dough, it is richer yet not as delicate as flaky pastry dough. It can be handled more than flaky pastry dough and can be rolled out or simply pressed into the pan.

In general, baking sheets and pans for kneaded dough do not have to be greased because of the amount of butter used in the dough. Some recipes, however, will call for greasing the pans because of the larger amounts of liquid in the recipes. Follow the directions in the recipes to assure easy removal of baked goods, then set aside to cool.

The Individual Steps

1 Sift the dry ingredients together.

2 Sift to loosen the flour and remove any lumps.

3 If cocoa is used in the recipe, sift it with the other ingredients.

1 Add the remaining ingredients in the order called for in the recipe.

2 If adding eggs, be sure to break them into a small cup or bowl to check for freshness.

3 Begin to combine the ingredients as you cut in the butter and shortening.

1 Combine ingredients using a pastry blender, a fork, or the dough hook of an electric mixer. If using dough hook, set first on lowest speed to blend ingredients, then set on highest speed to mix well.

2 Add the water called for by the tablespoonful stirring until a smooth dough is formed.

3 If fruit is called for in the recipe, add it last.

1 Turn the dough out onto a lightly floured board or pastry cloth.

2 To knead the dough, push it away from you with the heel of your hand.

3 Pull the outer edge toward the center.

4 Repeat the pushing and pulling motion until the dough is smooth.

5 Shape the dough into a ball.

6 Cover with plastic wrap and chill for 30 minutes.

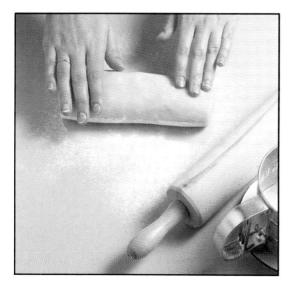

1 Sprinkle the work surface lightly with flour.

2 Begin to roll out the dough to the specified thickness.

3 Lift the rolling pin slightly as you roll out the edges. This will help to keep the dough from being thinner around the edges than in the middle.

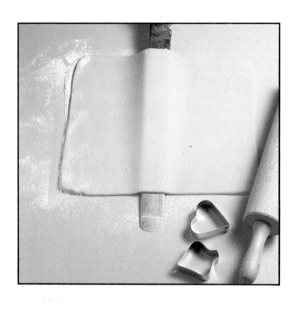

1 Slide a large knife under the dough occasionally to prevent sticking.

2 As you lift the dough with the knife, turn the dough ¼ turn to maintain an even thickness.

3 Try to roll the dough to the size called for in the recipe.

4 Trim the edges neatly with a knife, or fold into shape.

5 Roll slightly to seal.

1 Use a cookie cutter or sharp knife to cut out the desired shapes.

2 If you are lining a tart, flan, or pie pan, be sure to roll out the dough larger than the pan.

3 Trim any excess with a sharp knife or fold over and crimp.

4 You can also place the pan over the dough to check that the size is correct.

1 Roll out dough and fit into pan.

2 Or, press the dough into the pan.

3 Press it out evenly with your fingertips.

4 Prick the dough in several places with the tines of a fork.

Baking

Follow the instructions given in the recipes for baking. Be sure to have the oven at the correct temperature. Some recipes call for pre-baking the crust before the filling is added. In this case, the dough is placed in the baking pan, covered with foil, and then dried beans or pie weights are placed atop the foil. The crust is then baked for a short time, and the weights and foil are removed. The pie or flan is then filled and baked again. This helps to prevent soggy crusts. This procedure is also used to bake pie crusts for cream pies that will later be chilled. In this case, the pie weights and foil are removed after baking and the crust returned to the oven to brown for a short time before being filled.

Follow the directions given in the recipe for cooling the baked pie or pastry. Some are cooled in the pan while others are removed from the pan and cooled on a wire rack.

Cream Cheese Pastries

2 cups flour
2 teaspoons baking powder
1 teaspoon salt
1 teaspoon vanilla
1 8-ounce package cream cheese, softened and cut into small pieces
1 cup butter *or* margarine at room temperature
   Raspberry jam
1 cup confectioners' sugar
2 to 4 tablespoons hot water

Sift flour, baking powder, and salt into a large bowl. Add vanilla, cream cheese, and butter. Combine using a pastry blender, a fork, or the dough hook of an electric mixer. If using a dough hook, set first on lowest speed to blend, then set on highest speed to mix well.

Turn dough out onto a lightly floured board; knead until smooth. Roll out dough to a ¼-inch thickness. Fold by bringing bottom third up over half the dough, then bring the top piece down, letter-style. Roll out folded dough. Repeat the folding and rolling process two times. Cover dough and chill for 4 hours or overnight.

Preheat oven to 425°.

Roll out dough to a ¼-inch thickness about 12 x 6-inches long. Cut into 3-inch squares. Place 1 tablespoon of jam in the middle of each square. Fold into triangles; press edges together. Place on non-stick cookie sheet.

Bake for 15 minutes or until golden. Place on wire rack to cool. Combine sugar and water in small bowl until smooth. Drizzle over pastries.

Makes 8 servings

Apple Strudel

2 cups flour
¼ teaspoon salt
3 tablespoons vegetable oil
¾ cup hot water
    Apple Filling
¼ cup butter *or* margarine, melted
½ cup fine bread crumbs
    Confectioners' sugar

Preheat oven to 425°. Grease two 10 x 15-inch cookie sheets.

Sift flour and salt into a large bowl. Make a well in center. Blend in oil and water, a little at a time, using a pastry blender, fork, or the dough hook of an electric mixer. If using dough hook, set first on lowest speed to blend, then set on highest speed to mix well. Turn dough out onto a lightly floured board; knead until dough is smooth. Shape into a ball. Brush with oil; cover with plastic wrap. Chill for 30 minutes. Prepare Apple Filling.

Divide dough in half. Stretch each piece of dough slowly and carefully by using your knuckles on the underside of the dough. Work from the center to the outer edge until the dough is stretched to a 12 x 18-inch rectangle. Dough will be very thin. Trim off any uneven edges. Repeat with remaining dough.

Brush ½ the butter over each piece of dough. Sprinkle with bread crumbs, starting from a long side and leaving a 1-inch clean edge on the short sides. Spread ½ the Apple Filling over each piece of dough. Beginning with a long side, roll up each half, jelly-roll style. Press the ends together to seal.

Carefully place strudels on prepared cookie sheets. Brush with butter. Bake for 20 to 30 minutes, or until golden. Cool slightly on cookie sheet. Serve warm. Dust with confectioners' sugar.

Makes 2 strudels

Apple Filling

2 pounds firm cooking apples, peeled and sliced
1 tablespoon dark rum
2 tablespoons lemon juice
½ cup raisins
½ cup sugar

Place apples in large mixing bowl. Toss apples with rum and lemon juice. Stir in raisins and sugar; set aside.

Apple Crumb Flan

1½ cups flour
2 tablespoons sugar
½ teaspoon baking powder
¼ teaspoon salt
6 tablespoons butter *or* margarine at room temperature, cut into small pieces
2 tablespoons vegetable shortening
1 egg
4 to 7 tablespoons ice water
Apple Filling
Streusel Topping

Preheat oven to 425°. Lightly grease a 9-inch flan pan with removable bottom.

Sift flour, sugar, baking powder, and salt into a large bowl. Add butter, shortening, and egg. Combine using a pastry blender, a fork, or the dough hook of an electric mixer. If using dough hook, set first on lowest speed to blend, then set on highest speed to mix well. Add ice water by the tablespoonful while mixing until dough holds together. Shape into ball. Cover with plastic wrap and chill for 20 minutes. Press dough into pan base and sides. Prick dough several times with a fork.

Bake for 10 to 20 minutes or until golden. Set aside to cool. While dough is baking, prepare Apple Filling and Streusel Topping.

Spread cooled crust with Apple Filling; sprinkle with Streusel Topping. Bake for 30 minutes or until lightly browned. Cool in pan for 10 minutes; place on wire rack. Serve at room temperature.

Makes 8 servings

Apple Filling

2½ pounds firm cooking apples, peeled and sliced
½ cup sugar
½ teaspoon ground cinnamon
¼ cup butter

Place apples in large saucepan. Stir in remaining ingredients; simmer over medium heat, stirring often, until apples are barely tender. Set aside to cool.

Streusel Topping

1¼ cups flour
½ cup sugar
1 teaspoon vanilla
½ teaspoon ground cinnamon
¼ cup butter *or* margarine

Combine flour, sugar, vanilla, and cinnamon in a large bowl. Cut in butter using a pastry blender, a fork, or the dough hook of an electric mixer until mixture resembles crumbs.

Shortbread

1 cup butter *or* margarine at room temperature
½ cup sugar
2½ cups flour
1 egg, slightly beaten
Sugar

Preheat oven to 325°.

Cream butter and sugar in a large bowl until fluffy. Sift flour over butter, a little at a time, stirring until well blended. Stir in egg. Dough will be stiff. Press dough into a 9-inch square non-stick pan. Prick dough with a fork at 1-inch intervals. Sprinkle with sugar.

Bake 15 to 20 minutes or until golden brown. Cut into squares. Cool on wire rack. Store in an airtight container.

Makes approximately 16 squares

Fruit Tarts

2 cups flour
2 tablespoons sugar
¼ teaspoon salt
1 teaspoon vanilla
4 tablespoons butter *or* margarine at room temperature
3 tablespoons vegetable shortening
1 egg yolk, beaten with 1 tablespoon water
3 cups sliced fresh fruit (strawberries, raspberries, *or* bananas)
1½ cups currant jelly
¼ cup water

Sift flour, sugar, and salt into a large bowl. Add vanilla, butter, and shortening. Combine ingredients using a pastry blender, a fork, or the dough hook of an electric mixer. If using dough hook, set first on lowest speed to blend, then set on highest speed to mix well. Stir in egg while mixing until a smooth dough is formed. Add water, a tablespoonful at a time, if needed to make dough hold together. Shape dough into a ball. Cover with plastic wrap and chill for 20 minutes.

Preheat oven to 400°.

Turn out dough onto a lightly floured board. Roll out to a ¼-inch thickness. Cut out circles to fit 12 miniature tart pans; place circles in pans. Prick dough with fork. Cover tarts with foil; place a layer of pie weights or dried beans over foil.

Bake for 5 minutes. Remove foil and weights; continue baking for 5 to 7 minutes longer or until golden. Remove from oven; set aside to cool.

Arrange fruit in cooled tart shells. Heat jelly and ¼ cup water in saucepan over medium heat until mixture begins to boil, stirring often. Coat fruit with melted jelly.

Makes 12 servings

Vanilla Shortcake

2½ cups flour
1 teaspoon vanilla
¾ cup whipping cream
¾ cup butter *or* margarine at room temperature, cut into small pieces
¼ cup milk
½ cup sugar

Preheat oven to 400°.

Sift flour into a large bowl. Add vanilla, whipping cream, and butter; combine using a pastry blender, a fork, or the dough hook of an electric mixer. If using dough hook, set first on lowest speed to blend, then set to highest speed to mix well. Turn dough out onto a lightly floured board; knead until smooth. Shape into a ball. Cover with plastic wrap; chill for 15 minutes.

Press into a 9-inch square non-stick pan. Brush shortcake with milk and sprinkle with sugar. Bake for 20 minutes or until firm and golden brown. Cut into 2 x 2-inch squares. Remove from pan and place on wire rack to cool.

Makes approximately 16 squares

Cheese Pastries

2 cups flour
2 teaspoons baking powder
½ teaspoon salt, divided
1 8-ounce package cream cheese at room temperature, cut into ½-inch pieces
1 cup butter *or* margarine at room temperature, cut into ½-inch pieces
¼ cup milk
½ cup grated parmesan *or* Swiss cheese
¼ cup caraway seed
Coarsely ground green *or* red pepper

Sift flour, baking powder, and ¼ teaspoon salt into a large bowl. Add cream cheese and butter. Combine ingredients using a pastry blender, a fork, or the dough hook of an electric mixer. If using dough hook, set first on the lowest speed to blend, then set on highest speed to mix well.

Turn pastry out onto a lightly floured board. Knead dough until smooth. Roll out dough to a ¼-inch thickness. Fold by bringing bottom third up over half the dough, then bring top piece down letter-style. Repeat the rolling out and folding process two more times. Cover dough and chill for 4 hours or overnight.

Preheat oven to 425°. Roll out dough to ¼-inch thickness and cut into 2 x 3-inch rectangles. Brush with milk. Sprinkle with remaining salt, Parmesan cheese, caraway seed, and pepper.

Place pastries on a 10 x 15-inch non-stick cookie sheet. Bake for 10 minutes; serve hot.

Makes 8 servings

Cheese Cake

1½ cups flour
2 tablespoons sugar
½ teaspoon baking powder
¼ teaspoon salt
1 teaspoon vanilla
3 tablespoons butter *or* margarine at room temperature
3 tablespoons vegetable shortening
1 egg, slightly beaten
3 to 5 tablespoons ice water
Cream Cheese Filling
Crumb Topping

Sift flour, sugar, baking powder, and salt into a large bowl. Add vanilla, butter, and shortening; combine ingredients using a pastry blender, a fork, or the dough hook of an electric mixer. If using dough hook, set first on lowest speed to blend, then set on highest speed to mix well. Blend in egg; add water by the tablespoonful while mixing until dough holds together. Shape dough into a ball. Cover with plastic wrap and chill for 20 minutes.

Preheat oven to 425°. Use a 9-inch springform pan. Pat dough into pan, forming a 1-inch high rim around the sides. Prick dough several times with a fork. Bake for 10 minutes or until lightly browned; set aside to cool.

Prepare Cream Cheese Filling while crust is baking; pour into cooled crust. Reduce heat to 325°. Prepare Crumb Topping. Sprinkle Crumb Topping over filling.

Bake for 70 to 80 minutes or until firm. Turn off oven after baking, and open oven door. Leave the cake in oven for 2 hours or until completely cool. Chill for 12 hours before serving.

Makes 8 to 10 servings

Cream Cheese Filling

3 8-ounce packages cream cheese at room temperature
¾ cup sugar
3 tablespoons lemon juice
4 tablespoons cornstarch
3 eggs, separated
1 cup whipping cream

Combine cream cheese, sugar, lemon juice, cornstarch, and egg yolks in a large bowl. Beat for 5 to 10 minutes or until creamy and fluffy. Beat egg whites in a large bowl until stiff peaks form. Whip cream until stiff peaks form. Fold egg whites and whipped cream into cheese mixture.

Crumb Topping

¾ cup flour
⅓ cup sugar
1 teaspoon vanilla
¼ cup butter *or* margarine

Combine flour, sugar, and vanilla in a large bowl. Cut in butter using a pastry blender, a fork, or the dough hook of an electric mixer until mixture resembles crumbs.

Cheese Cake, this page

Poppy Seed & Apple Tart

2 cups flour
¾ cup sugar, divided
1 teaspoon baking powder
¼ teaspoon salt
1 teaspoon vanilla
6 tablespoons butter *or* margarine at room temperature
2 tablespoons vegetable shortening
1 cup lightly roasted ground hazelnuts
1 egg
4 to 6 tablespoons ice water
Poppy Seed Filling
2 pounds cooking apples, peeled and thinly sliced
1 teaspoon ground cinnamon

Sift flour, ¼ cup sugar, baking powder, and salt into a large bowl. Add vanilla, butter, shortening, and hazelnuts. Combine using a pastry blender, a fork, or the dough hook of an electric mixer. If using the dough hook, set first on lowest speed to blend, then set on highest speed to mix well. Blend in egg; add water by the tablespoonful while mixing until dough holds together.

Shape dough into a ball. Cover with plastic wrap; chill for 30 minutes. While dough is chilling, prepare Poppy Seed Filling. Simmer apples in a saucepan with remaining sugar and cinnamon just until tender; set aside.

Preheat oven to 400°. Grease a 9-inch springform pan.

Press or pat dough into bottom of prepared pan, forming a rim ¾ the way up the sides of the pan. Spread apples over the dough. Pour Poppy Seed Filling over apples.

Bake for 40 minutes or until a wooden skewer inserted in center comes out clean. Cool in oven with door open for 2 hours. Serve at room temperature or chill before serving.

Makes 8 to 10 servings

Poppy Seed Filling

1½ cups poppy seed
¾ cup hot milk
¼ cup butter *or* margarine
4 eggs, slightly beaten
2 cups milk, scalded
1 teaspoon vanilla
¼ teaspoon salt

Combine poppy seed, hot milk, and butter in a bowl. Set aside to cool for 30 minutes. Combine eggs, scalded milk, vanilla, and salt in a bowl. Stir in poppy seed mixture; set aside.

Apple Pie

2 cups flour
3 tablespoons vegetable shortening
4 tablespoons butter *or* margarine
¼ teaspoon salt
1 teaspoon grated lemon zest
4 to 6 tablespoons ice water
Apple Filling
1 egg white, slightly beaten
3 tablespoons sugar

Sift flour into a large bowl. Cut in shortening and butter with a pastry blender, a fork, or the dough hook of an electric mixer. If using dough hook, set first on lowest speed to blend, then set on highest speed to mix well. Blend in salt and lemon zest. Add ice water by the tablespoonful while mixing until dough holds together. Shape dough into a smooth ball. Cover with plastic wrap and chill for 1 hour. Prepare Apple Filling while dough is chilling.

Divide dough in half; turn out 1 piece onto a lightly floured board. Roll out dough to fit a 9-inch pie pan; place in pan. Pour Apple Filling into prepared crust. Roll out remaining dough on lightly floured board. Fold in half for easy handling and unfold crust over pie; crimp edges together. Prick top crust with tines of fork; cut a ½-inch hole in center of crust. Brush crust with egg white and sprinkle with sugar.

Bake 45 minutes or until crust is golden brown. Cool on wire rack.

Makes 6 servings

Apple Filling

3 pounds firm cooking apples, peeled and sliced
⅓ cup flour
½ cup sugar
½ teaspoon ground cinnamon
½ teaspoon ground nutmeg
½ cup golden raisins
2 tablespoons butter *or* margarine, cut into small pieces

Toss apples in a large bowl with remaining ingredients.

Apple Custard Pie

1½ cups flour
¼ teaspoon salt
½ cup vegetable shortening
1 egg yolk
4 to 5 tablespoons ice water
2 teaspoons lemon juice
1 cup peeled and thinly
   sliced cooking apples
⅓ cup sugar
½ teaspoon ground
   cinnamon
¼ teaspoon ground nutmeg
4 eggs, slightly beaten
2 cups milk, heated until
   very warm
1 teaspoon vanilla
¼ teaspoon salt

Preheat oven to 400°.

Sift flour and salt into a large bowl. Cut in shortening with a pastry blender until pieces are the size of small peas. Blend in egg yolk, 4 tablespoons ice water, and lemon juice using a pastry blender, a fork, or the dough hook of an electric mixer. Mix lightly until dough holds together. Add more water, if needed.

Shape dough into a ball. Place dough on a lightly floured board; roll outward from center into a ⅛-inch thick circle, about 10 inches in diameter. Loosely fit dough into a 9-inch pie pan. Trim edges and flute as desired.

Arrange apple slices in crust. Combine 1 tablespoon sugar with cinnamon and nutmeg. Sprinkle over apples. Beat together eggs, remaining sugar, milk, vanilla, and salt. Place pie on oven rack. Pour egg mixture over apples. Bake for 30 minutes or until a wooden skewer inserted in center comes out clean. Cool or chill pie before serving.

Makes 6 to 8 servings

Half-Moon Cookies

¾ cup butter *or* margarine at
   room temperature
¾ cup confectioners' sugar
1 teaspoon almond extract
1½ cups ground almonds
2½ cups flour

Preheat oven to 325°. Lightly grease a 10 x 15-inch cookie sheet.

Cream butter and sugar in a large bowl until light and fluffy. Blend in almond extract and ground almonds. Sift flour over batter; stir until blended.

Knead dough lightly and shape into a ball. Pinch off a tablespoonful of dough at a time. Roll each ball of dough between your palms to form a 2-inch long pencil-shaped roll. Place each roll on prepared cookie sheet; curve ends into half-moon shape. Continue until all the dough has been used.

Bake for 10 to 12 minutes or until golden. Remove from pan and place on wire rack to cool.

Makes approximately 30 cookies

Ring Cookies

2 cups flour
½ teaspoon baking powder
¼ teaspoon salt
¾ cup butter *or* margarine, chilled and cut into small pieces
¾ cup whipping cream
2 teaspoons vanilla
　Milk
1 10-ounce jar raspberry jam
1 teaspoon raspberry liqueur, optional
　Confectioners' sugar

Sift flour, baking powder, and salt into a large bowl. Cut in butter using a pastry blender, a fork, or the dough hook of an electric mixer. If using dough hook, set first on lowest speed to blend, then set on highest speed to mix well. Stir in cream and vanilla with fork until dough holds together. Shape into a ball. Cover with plastic wrap and chill for 1 hour.

Preheat oven to 375°.

Roll out dough on a lightly floured board to a ¼-inch thickness. Cut out thirty 3-inch circles with a cookie cutter. Cut out centers of half the cookies with a 1-inch cookie cutter to form ring; discard centers. Place whole cookies and ring-shaped cookies on a 10 x 15-inch non-stick cookie sheet. Brush with milk. Bake for 10 to 15 minutes or until golden. Set aside to cool.

Blend jam and liqueur until smooth. Spread a thin coat of jam mixture over the whole cookies. Top with ring-shaped cookies; fill open centers with jam mixture. Dust with confectioners' sugar.

Makes 15 cookies

Hazelnut Slices

3 cups flour, sifted
4 tablespoons cornstarch
2 teaspoons baking powder
1¼ cups sugar
1 teaspoon vanilla
¼ teaspoon salt
1 cup butter *or* margarine, chilled and cut into small pieces
2 cups chopped hazelnuts
2 eggs

Sift flour, cornstarch, and baking powder into a large bowl. Mix in sugar, vanilla, and salt. Cut in butter using a pastry blender, a fork, or the dough hook of an electric mixer until well blended. Stir in nuts. Blend in eggs with a fork until mixture holds together.

Shape dough into a ball. Shape into a log 3 inches in diameter and wrap in plastic wrap. Chill for at least 1 hour.

Preheat oven to 375°.

Cut the log into ½-inch thick slices; place on a 10 x 15-inch non-stick cookie sheet. Bake for 10 to 15 minutes or until golden. Set aside to cool.

Makes 10 to 12 servings

Linzer Tart

1 cup flour
¾ cup ground almonds
½ cup sugar
1 teaspoon ground cinnamon
¼ teaspoon ground cloves
¼ teaspoon salt
   Zest of 1 lemon
3 egg yolks
1 teaspoon vanilla
1 cup butter *or* margarine at room temperature, cut into ½-inch pieces
1 cup raspberry jam

Preheat oven to 350°.

Combine first 9 ingredients in a large bowl. Cut in butter, a little bit at a time, using a pastry blender, a fork, or the dough hook of an electric mixer. If using dough hook, set first on lowest speed to blend, then set on highest speed to mix well. Loosely pat ⅔ of the dough into an ungreased 9-inch springform pan, forming a ¾-inch rim around the sides. Chill remaining dough.

Spread raspberry jam evenly over dough. Roll out remaining dough between 2 sheets of waxed paper to a ½-inch thickness. Cut into 10 strips, ½ to ¾-inch wide. Arrange 3 to 5 strips evenly spaced over top. Rotate pan and place 3 to 5 more strips evenly spaced across top, forming a lattice design.

Bake 45 to 50 minutes or until golden brown. Remove from oven and set aside for 5 minutes; remove sides of pan. Cool to room temperature before serving.

Makes 8 servings

Pretzels

1⅓ cups sifted flour
¼ cup sugar
   Zest of ½ lemon
½ cup butter *or* margarine, chilled and cut into small pieces
1 egg, lightly beaten
1 cup finely chopped almonds
1 egg white, lightly beaten

Combine flour, sugar, and lemon zest in a large bowl. Cut in butter with a pastry blender or two knives until consistency of coarse crumbs. Stir in egg; blend well. Form dough into a ball. On a lightly floured surface, knead dough until smooth. Do not overwork dough. Form into a ball. Flatten slightly; cover in plastic wrap. Chill for at least 2 hours.

Break off tablespoonsful of dough and roll out on a lightly floured surface to form 10-inch ropes. Twist ropes into pretzels. Place on non-stick cookie sheets. Chill for 20 minutes.

Preheat oven to 375°.

Brush tops of pretzels with egg white; sprinkle with chopped almonds. Bake for 10 to 12 minutes or until barely golden. Remove from baking sheet and cool on a wire rack.

Makes approximately 2 dozen

Linzer Tart, this page

Fancy Fruit Tart

1½ cups flour
2 tablespoons sugar
¼ teaspoon salt
3 tablespoons butter *or* margarine, chilled and cut into small pieces
3 tablespoons vegetable shortening
1 egg
2 teaspoons lemon juice
3 to 5 tablespoons ice water
1 egg, slightly beaten
  Cream Filling
4 to 5 cups sliced fruit (strawberries, raspberries, *or* bananas)
1 cup currant jelly
3 tablespoons water

Sift flour, sugar, and salt into a large bowl. Cut in butter and shortening, a little at a time, using a pastry blender, a fork, or the dough hook of an electric mixer. If using dough hook, set first on lowest speed to blend, then set on highest speed to mix well. Add egg, lemon juice, and water while mixing until dough holds together. Shape dough into a ball. Flatten slightly and cover with plastic wrap. Chill for 30 minutes.

Preheat oven to 375°.

On a lightly floured surface, roll out dough into a 9-inch circle. Fold in half and carefully ease into flan pan with removable bottom. Press dough into bottom and sides of pan.

Line crust with foil. Place dried beans or pastry weights over foil. Bake for 7 minutes. Remove beans and foil. Brush bottom and sides with beaten egg. Return crust to oven for 8 to 10 minutes or until lightly browned. Cool completely.

Prepare Cream Filling while crust is baking. Spread filling over cooled crust. Top with fruit. Melt currant jelly and water in small saucepan, stirring often. Brush fruit with glaze.

For best results, assemble the tart close to serving time.

Makes 8 servings

Cream Filling

1 cup milk
3 egg yolks
⅓ cup sugar
½ teaspoon vanilla
2 tablespoons cornstarch
2 tablespoons butter *or* margarine

Bring milk to a boil in a saucepan; set aside to cool. Beat egg yolks, sugar, and vanilla in a bowl until thickened; stir in cornstarch. Stir in milk in a slow, steady stream until blended. Return mixture to saucepan and bring to a boil, stirring constantly, until thickened and mixture will coat a spoon. Remove from heat; beat in butter. Set aside to cool.

Filled Cookies

2½ cups flour
⅓ cup sugar
1 teaspoon baking powder
¼ teaspoon salt
½ cup **butter** *or* **margarine at room temperature, cut into small pieces**
1 egg
1 teaspoon vanilla
2 tablespoons milk
Filling
Glaze

Sift flour, sugar, baking powder, and salt together into a large bowl. Cut in butter, a few pieces at a time, using a pastry blender, a fork, or the dough hook of an electric mixer. Stir in egg, vanilla, and milk with a fork until dough holds together. Shape dough into a ball. Flatten dough slightly and cover with plastic wrap. Chill for 30 minutes.

Preheat oven to 400°. Roll out dough to a ¼-inch thickness on a lightly floured board. Use a 1½-inch cookie cutter to cut out circles. Place circles on a 10 x 15-inch non-stick cookie sheet. Bake for 10 minutes or until golden. Prepare Filling while cookies are baking. Remove cookies from pan and place on wire rack to cool.

Spread Filling onto the bottoms of half the cookies; top with remaining cookies. Prepare the Glaze. Dip the ends of the cookies into the glaze; place on wire rack for 30 minutes or until glaze hardens.

Makes 2 dozen cookies

Filling

½ cup **butter** *or* **margarine**
¾ cup confectioners' sugar
1 heaping teaspoon cocoa
1 teaspoon vanilla

Cream butter until fluffy. Blend in remaining ingredients; mix well.

Glaze

3 ounces semi-sweet chocolate
1 tablespoon **butter** *or* **margarine**

Melt chocolate and butter in top of a double boiler over simmering water; stir until blended.

Hazelnut Ring

2½ cups flour
2 teaspoons baking powder
½ cup sugar
¼ teaspoon salt
1 teaspoon vanilla
½ cup butter *or* margarine,
  chilled and cut into small
  pieces
1 egg
4 to 6 tablespoons milk
  Hazelnut Filling
1 egg yolk
1 tablespoon milk

Sift flour, baking powder, sugar, and salt into a large bowl. Add vanilla and butter. Combine using a pastry blender, a fork, or the dough hook of an electric mixer. If using dough hook, set first on lowest speed to blend, then set on highest speed to mix well. Blend in egg and 4 tablespoons milk while mixing until dough holds together. Add more milk, if needed. Shape dough into a ball. Cover with plastic wrap; chill for 20 minutes. Prepare Hazelnut Filling while dough is chilling.

Preheat oven to 375°. Grease a 10 x 15-inch cookie sheet.

Roll out dough on a lightly floured board into a 10 x 14-inch rectangle. Spread with Hazelnut Filling. Roll up dough, jelly-roll style, beginning on a long side. Place on prepared cookie sheet and shape into a ring; press ends together.

Beat egg yolk and milk together in a small bowl; brush ring with mixture. Bake for 45 minutes or until golden; set aside to cool.

Makes 8 servings

Hazelnut Filling

2 cups ground hazelnuts
½ cup sugar
½ teaspoon almond extract
½ egg yolk
1 egg white
4 to 6 tablespoons water

Combine all ingredients in a bowl until mixture is smooth and spreadable.

Hazelnut Ring, this page

Tangy Filled Tarts

1 cup flour
2 tablespoons sugar
¼ teaspoon salt
6 tablespoons butter *or* margarine at room temperature, cut into small pieces
1 teaspoon lemon juice
2 tablespoons ice water
  Plum Filling *or* Rhubarb Filling

To make the tart shell, sift flour, sugar and salt into a large bowl. Add butter. Combine using a pastry blender, a fork, or the dough hook of an electric mixer. If using a dough hook, set first on lowest speed to blend, then set to high speed to mix well. Add lemon juice and 1 tablespoon water; toss lightly with a fork. Add remaining 1 tablespoon water and mix until dough holds together. Shape dough into a ball. Flatten slightly and cover with plastic wrap; chill for at least 2 hours.

Roll out dough on a lightly floured surface to form a 9-inch circle. Fold in half and carefully ease into an 8-inch flan ring or cake pan with removable bottom. Press dough onto bottom and sides of pan. Patch dough, if necessary, by moistening with a little water and pressing edges together. Chill for 30 minutes.

Preheat oven to 375°. Line unbaked shell with aluminum foil. Fill shell with pie weights or dried beans. Bake for 20 minutes or until edges begin to brown. Remove weights and foil. Return shell to oven for 8 to 10 minutes or until lightly browned. If shell is to be used with a fruit filling, brush a lightly beaten egg over bottom and sides before returning to oven.

Remove from oven and let stand 3 to 4 minutes to cool slightly. If using flan ring, cool completely in pan on baking sheet. If using a cake pan, carefully remove rim. Transfer shell, still on pan bottom, to wire rack and cool.

Prepare Plum or Rhubarb Filling. Fill baked shell as directed.

Makes 1 shell

Plum Filling

2 tablespoons currant jelly
¼ cup sugar
¼ cup water
6 to 8 plums, halved and
    pitted
1 tablespoon arrowroot
1 tablespoon sugar
1 tablespoon Kirsch
    Whipped cream

Brush melted jelly over bottom and sides of tart shell; set aside. Heat sugar and water in a small saucepan, stirring until sugar dissolves; set aside.

Place plums in a medium saucepan or skillet in a single layer. Pour sugar water over plums. Bring to a boil. Reduce heat; simmer until tender but firm. Remove plums to a large platter with a slotted spoon.

Combine arrowroot and sugar; stir in ⅔ cup cooled pan juices. Bring to a boil, stirring constantly. Reduce heat. Add Kirsch. Cook and stir until sauce is thick and clear. Remove from heat.

Arrange plums, curved sides up, in tart shell. Pour sauce over plums. Refrigerate until chilled. Serve with whipped cream.

Makes 6 servings

Rhubarb Filling

2 cups rhubarb, cut into
    2-inch pieces
⅓ cup sugar
    Pastry Cream

Combine rhubarb and sugar in a heavy saucepan. Cook over low heat, stirring occasionally, until rhubarb is tender but firm. Remove from heat. Let stand until cool.

Prepare Pastry Cream and fill tart shell. Arrange rhubarb on top of Pastry Cream in a single layer. Serve at once.

Makes 6 servings

Pastry Cream

1 cup milk
3 egg yolks
⅓ cup sugar
¼ teaspoon vanilla
2 tablespoons cornstarch
2 tablespoons butter *or*
    margarine, optional
    Orange liqueur

Bring milk to a boil in a small saucepan. Cover and set aside. Beat egg yolks, sugar and vanilla in a bowl until thick and light-colored. Stir in cornstarch. Stir hot milk into egg mixture in a slow, steady stream. Return to saucepan and bring to a boil, stirring constantly, until thick and mixture coats a spoon. Remove from heat. Stir in butter, if desired. Flavor to taste with orange liqueur.

Streusel Cookies

2 cups flour
½ cup sugar
1 teaspoon baking powder
1 teaspoon vanilla
¼ teaspoon salt
¾ cup butter *or* margarine, chilled and cut into small pieces
¾ cup blanched, ground almonds
Streusel Topping
Candied cherries

Sift flour, sugar, and baking powder into a large bowl. Mix in vanilla and salt. Cut in butter using a pastry blender, a fork, or the dough hook of an electric mixer. If using dough hook, set first on lowest speed to blend, then set on highest speed to mix well. Stir in almonds. Shape into a ball. Cover with plastic wrap and chill for 1 hour. Prepare Streusel Topping while dough is chilling.

Preheat oven to 375°.

Roll out dough on lightly floured board to a ¼-inch thickness. Use a 2-inch round cookie cutter to cut dough into circles. Place circles on a 10 x 15-inch non-stick cookie sheet.

Spread Streusel Topping evenly over the cookies. Top with candied cherries. Bake for 15 minutes or until golden. Cool on wire rack before serving.

Makes approximately 3 dozen cookies

Streusel Topping

1½ cups flour
¾ cup sugar
1 teaspoon vanilla
½ teaspoon ground cinnamon
½ cup butter *or* margarine, chilled and cut into small pieces

Combine flour, sugar, vanilla, and cinnamon in a large bowl. Cut in butter using a pastry blender, a fork, or the dough hook of an electric mixer until mixture resembles crumbs.

Streusel Cookies, this page

Peanut Cookies

2 cups flour
¼ cup sugar
½ teaspoon baking powder
¼ teaspoon salt
6 tablespoons butter *or* margarine, cut into small pieces
2 tablespoons vegetable shortening
1 egg
3 to 6 tablespoons water
Peanut Filling
4 ounces semi-sweet chocolate

Sift flour, sugar, baking powder, and salt into a large bowl. Cut in butter and shortening using a pastry blender, a fork, or the dough hook of an electric mixer. If using dough hook, set first on lowest speed to blend, then set on highest speed to mix well. Stir in egg and add water by the tablespoonful until mixture holds together. Shape into a ball. Cover with plastic wrap and chill for 1 hour. While dough is chilling, prepare Peanut Filling.

Preheat oven to 375°. Roll out dough onto a 9 x 13-inch non-stick cookie sheet. Spread Peanut Filling over dough.

Bake for 20 minutes or until golden. Cool in pan; cut into squares or rectangles.

Melt chocolate in top of double boiler over simmering water; stir until smooth. Spread chocolate over cooled cookies. Set aside for 30 minutes or until chocolate hardens.

Makes 2 dozen cookies

Peanut Filling

1¼ cups unsalted, coarsely ground peanuts
½ cup almond paste (available at gourmet stores)
¼ cup sugar
3 tablespoons butter *or* margarine at room temperature
1 egg white
3 tablespoons dark rum

Combine all ingredients in a large bowl; blend well.

Fudgy Tarts

1 cup flour
¼ teaspoon baking powder
¼ teaspoon salt
½ cup shortening
1 egg, beaten
   Fudge Filling
24 small pecan halves

Sift flour, baking powder, and salt together into large bowl. Cut in shortening, using pastry blender or fork, until mixture resembles coarse crumbs. Pour egg over mixture. Stir until dough clings together. Form into a ball; cover with plastic wrap. Chill for 1 hour.

Preheat oven to 350°.

Roll out dough on lightly floured board to ⅛-inch thickness. Using a 2½-inch cookie cutter, cut out 24 circles. Press into miniature muffin cups. Chill for 10 minutes. Prepare Fudge Filling.

Place 1 scant tablespoon filling in each cup; top with pecan half. Bake 20 to 25 minutes. Cool; remove from pans. Store in refrigerator.

Makes 2 dozen tarts

Fudge Filling

1 6-ounce package semi-sweet chocolate chips
½ cup sugar
1 tablespoon milk
1 tablespoon butter *or* margarine
1 teaspoon instant coffee
1 teaspoon vanilla *or* rum extract
1 egg, beaten

Melt chocolate in saucepan; remove from heat. Stir in remaining ingredients.

Checkerboard Cookies

¾ cup butter *or* margarine at
    room temperature
2 cups flour
½ cup sugar
2 egg yolks
2 tablespoons cocoa
1 tablespoon water
½ teaspoon vanilla
1 egg white, beaten with
    1 tablespoon water

Beat butter, flour, sugar, and egg yolks in a large bowl until creamy. Divide the dough in half; blend cocoa and water into half the dough. Blend vanilla into the remaining dough. On a lightly floured surface, roll out each dough into a ¼-inch thick, 10 x 12-inch rectangle.

To create a checkerboard pattern, cut six ½-inch wide strips from the light dough. Cut six ½-inch wide strips from the dark dough. Use either the remaining light or dark dough as a base. Place the cut-out strips on the base, alternating colors, with 3 rows of 4 strips on top of each other. Brush with egg white. Wrap the dough base around the strips to form a roll. Cover with plastic wrap and chill for 45 minutes.

Preheat oven to 375°. Lightly grease a 10 x 15-inch cookie sheet.

Cut rolls into ¼ to ½-inch thick slices. Place on prepared cookie sheet. Bake for 5 to 10 minutes. Remove from cookie sheet and cool on rack.

Variation: To create a combination cookie design, cut a ½-inch wide strip from the dark dough; brush it with egg white. Wrap both dark and light dough around the dark strip. Chill, slice, and bake as directed above.

Makes 2 to 3 dozen cookies

Almond Slices

1½ cups sliced unblanched
    almonds
2 cups flour
1 cup sugar
1 teaspoon ground
    cinnamon
2 eggs
1 cup butter *or* margarine at
    room temperature

Combine almonds, flour, sugar, and cinnamon in large bowl. Add eggs; blend well. Cut in butter using a pastry blender or wooden spoon; mix until dough clings together. Divide dough in half; shape dough into two long blocks, each 3 inches wide. Cover in plastic wrap; chill overnight.

Preheat oven to 375°. Cut dough into ⅛-inch thick slices. Place slices about 1 inch apart on a 10 x 15-inch cookie sheet. Bake for 10 minutes or until edges are lightly browned. Remove from cookie sheet; place on wire rack to cool.

Fresh Orange Pie

Sweet Crust
½ cup red currant jelly
4 oranges, peeled and
sectioned

Prepare Sweet Crust. In a small saucepan, melt jelly over low heat; cool slightly. Brush bottom of cooled crust lightly with melted jelly. Arrange orange sections in crust. Brush with remaining jelly.

Makes 8 servings

Sweet Crust

2 cups flour
½ cup sugar
¼ teaspoon salt
2 egg yolks
1 teaspoon grated lemon
   zest
¾ cup butter *or* margarine

Sift together flour, sugar, and salt in a medium bowl. Stir in egg yolks and lemon zest with a fork. Use fingers to blend in butter until mixture holds together. Form into a ball. Cover with plastic wrap. Chill for 30 minutes or until firm.
   Preheat oven to 400°.
   Roll out dough on a lightly floured surface to form a 12-inch circle. (Pastry will be fairly thick.) Fit dough into a 9-inch fluted tart pan with a removable bottom. Prick well with a fork.
   Line crust with foil; fill with pie weights or dried beans. Bake for 6 minutes. Remove foil and weights. Return to oven; bake 6 to 7 minutes or until pastry is lightly browned. Cool in pan on a wire rack. Gently remove from pan and place on a serving plate.

Black Russian Pie

Butter Crust
⅓ cup coffee-flavored
   liqueur
2 envelopes unflavored
   gelatin
½ cup milk
2 eggs
½ cup sugar
⅔ cup vodka
1½ cups whipping cream
   Chocolate curls, optional

Prepare Butter Crust; set aside until cool. Pour coffee liqueur into a blender or food processor. Add gelatin; let stand 5 minutes.
   In a small saucepan, heat milk to boiling; pour over gelatin mixture. Blend until gelatin dissolves. Add eggs, sugar, and vodka; blend until smooth. Cool until mixture begins to thicken.
   Beat whipping cream in a large mixing bowl until stiff peaks form. Fold gelatin mixture into whipped cream. Chill until mixture mounds slightly. Pour into prepared piecrust.
   Chill until firm, about 4 hours. Garnish with chocolate curls, if desired.

Makes 6 to 8 servings

Butter Crust

½ cup butter *or* margarine at
   room temperature
2 tablespoons sugar
1 cup flour

Preheat oven to 375°.
   Combine butter and sugar in a mixing bowl; blend well. Add flour; mix on low speed just until dough holds together. Press dough into a 9-inch pie pan. Bake for 12 to 15 minutes or until light golden brown.

Makes one 9-inch crust

Tea Cookies

2 cups flour
⅓ cup sugar
1 teaspoon baking powder
¼ teaspoon salt
1 teaspoon vanilla
½ cup butter *or* margarine,
   chilled and cut into small
   pieces
1 egg

Combine flour, sugar, baking powder, and salt in a large bowl. Stir in vanilla. Cut in butter, a few pieces at a time, using a pastry blender, a fork, or the dough hook of an electric mixer. If using dough hook, set first on lowest speed to blend, then set on highest speed to mix well. Stir in egg with fork until dough holds together. Shape into a ball. Cover with plastic wrap and chill for 30 minutes.
   A variety of cookies can be made from this basic dough.
   Form 6-inch long pencil-shaped ropes from the dough. Twist each rope into pretzel shapes. Brush with milk, sprinkle with sugar, and place on a 10 x 15-inch non-stick cookie sheet. Bake for 8 to 10 minutes or until golden. Remove from cookie sheet and cool on wire rack.
Variations: Roll out dough on lightly floured board to a ¼-inch thickness. Cut into 2-inch circles with cookie cutter; place on cookie sheet. Bake for 8 to 10 minutes; cool on wire rack. Spread ½ the cookies with jam or jelly; top with remaining cookies. Dust with confectioners' sugar.
   Roll out dough as directed above. Cut into circles. Place on cookie sheet and brush with milk. Sprinkle with sugar or slivered almonds. Bake for 8 to 10 minutes. Cool on wire rack.

Makes approximately 2 dozen cookies

Plum Crumb Tart

2 cups flour
¼ teaspoon baking powder
¼ teaspoon salt
¼ cup butter *or* margarine,
  cut into small pieces
4 tablespoons vegetable
  shortening
4 to 6 tablespoons boiling
  water
2 cups fine bread crumbs
2 pounds small plums,
  halved
½ cup raisins
½ cup plum jelly *or* currant
  jelly
3 tablespoons water

Sift flour, baking powder, and salt into a large bowl. Add butter and shortening. Combine using a pastry blender, a fork, or the dough hook of an electric mixer. If using dough hook, set first on lowest speed to blend, then set to highest speed to mix well. Add boiling water by the tablespoonful while mixing until dough holds together. Shape dough into a ball. Cover with plastic wrap and chill for 30 minutes.

Preheat oven to 350°. Lightly grease a 9-inch springform pan, or 9-inch square pan. Roll out dough or pat dough into bottom of prepared pan, forming a ½-inch high rim around the sides.

Sprinkle bread crumbs over dough. Arrange plum halves slightly overlapping across the dough. Sprinkle with raisins. Bake for 45 minutes or until crust is golden.

While tart is baking, melt jelly and 3 tablespoons water in a small saucepan; stir to combine. Brush tart with melted jelly; set aside to cool.

Makes 8 servings

Strudel

1 cup butter *or* margarine at
  room temperature
2 cups flour
¼ teaspoon salt
1 cup sour cream
¼ cup fine, dry bread
  crumbs
1⅓ cups pineapple, orange, *or*
  apricot marmalade
1 cup flaked coconut
1 cup golden raisins
1 cup chopped nuts
½ cup halved maraschino
  cherries
  Confectioners' sugar

Cream butter in a large bowl until fluffy. Sift together flour and salt; blend into butter. Blend in sour cream, a little at a time, using pastry blender, fork, or the dough hook of an electric mixer. If using dough hook on electric mixer, set first on lowest speed to blend, then set on highest speed to mix well.

Divide dough into 4 equal portions. Cover each with plastic wrap; chill for 3 hours. Roll out dough, 1 portion at a time, into 15 x 12-inch rectangles on a lightly floured board.

Sprinkle 1 tablespoon crumbs on each rectangle. Spread each rectangle with ⅓ cup marmalade; ¼ cup each coconut, raisins, and nuts; and ⅛ cup cherries. Roll each rectangle jelly-roll style, beginning on a long side; pinch ends to seal.

Preheat oven to 350°. Grease 10 x 15-inch cookie sheets.

Place rolls on prepared cookie sheets. Slash top of each roll diagonally into 12 slices. Bake for 35 minutes or until golden. Place on waxed paper; slice immediately. Cool slightly before serving; dust with confectioners' sugar. Store loosely covered with waxed paper or foil.

Makes 4 dozen slices

Fruit & Cheese Tarts

½ cup butter *or* margarine at
    room temperature
1 5-ounce jar cheese spread
    at room temperature
1½ cups flour
    Fruit Filling

Combine butter and cheese spread in large bowl. Cut in flour using a pastry blender or fork; blend just until dough clings together. Shape into a roll 1¼ inches in diameter; cover with plastic wrap. Chill for 1 hour.

Preheat oven to 375°.

Cut roll into 72 ⅛-inch thick slices. Place 1 slice in bottom of each of 12 muffin cups. Arrange 5 slices around sides of each cup, overlapping slightly. Prick dough on bottom and sides with fork.

Bake for 18 to 20 minutes; place on wire rack to cool. Carefully remove tarts from pan. Prepare Fruit Filling. Spoon filling into tarts just before serving.

Makes 1 dozen tarts

Fruit Filling

¼ cup sugar
2 tablespoons cornstarch
1 8-ounce can crushed
    pineapple, drained and
    juice reserved
1 11-ounce can mandarin
    oranges, drained, ½ cup
    juice reserved
1 tablespoon lemon juice

Combine sugar, cornstarch, pineapple juice, mandarin orange juice and lemon juice in saucepan. Cook over medium heat, stirring until thickened. Stir in fruit. Chill for 1 hour.

Breads, Rolls, and Pastries

Breads, Rolls, and Pastries

How to bake breads, rolls, and pastries with yeast is not a mystery known only to professional chefs. The secret is simply to combine the yeast with dry ingredients and warm liquid, set the mixture in a warm place, and allow the "magic" process of "rising" to begin. The gas which yeast gives off when mixed with other ingredients leavens the dough.

Using packages of active dry yeast rather than cake-style yeast makes the process even simpler. The packages can be sprinkled directly onto the flour and carefully mixed in with the other ingredients and a warm liquid. Exceptions to this method are dough with rich ingredients such as Babas au Rhum and stollens. For these special recipes, the yeast works best if mixed with warm liquid first.

For most recipes, grease baking pans with softened butter or margarine and dust with flour or fine bread crumbs.

The Individual Steps

Method 1:
Combining the flour and yeast before adding warm liquid.

1 Sift flour into a large bowl.

2 Sprinkle with yeast. Dry yeast has the advantage of being able to be mixed directly with the flour before adding the warm liquid which starts the leavening process.

1 Blend in the ingredients called for in the recipe, including the warm liquid. For best results, the liquid should be lukewarm (about 110°-120°).

2 Stir liquids into the dry ingredients gradually, so the warmth is evenly distributed throughout the dough.

3 Combine the ingredients with a wooden spoon or the dough hook of an electric mixer. If using mixer, begin on the lowest setting to blend and then adjust to high for 5 minutes until thoroughly combined.

Method 2:
Combining the yeast and warm liquid before adding to the flour and other ingredients.

1 Combine the cream, yeast, and sugar in a large bowl.

2 Set aside for 15 minutes to begin the leavening process.

1 Sift the flour into a large bowl and make a hollow in it.

2 Add the yeast liquid and the other ingredients called for in the recipe.

3 Combine the ingredients using a wooden spoon or the dough hook of an electric mixer. If using mixer, begin on the lowest setting to blend, then adjust the mixer to high for 5 minutes until thoroughly combined.

4 If the dough becomes sticky, add a little more flour, but not too much as the dough must remain moderately soft.

1 Knead the dough on a lightly floured board until smooth.

2 Knead the dough with the heel of your hands in a push-pull motion to assure an even blending of all the ingredients.

3 Place the dough in a greased bowl.

4 Turn once to grease lightly.

1 Cover the dough or pan with a dish towel.

2 Set aside in a warm place that is free of drafts. An excellent place to use is the oven.

3 Preheat the oven to about 125° for 2 minutes.

4 Turn the oven off, place the dough in the oven, and close the door.

5 Or, you may place the dough in the oven with just the oven light turned on.

1 Punch dough down.

2 Turn it into the prepared pan, roll it out, shape it, or braid it as called for in the recipe.

3 In most cases, the dough will then be set aside in a warm, draft-free area to again double in bulk before baking.

Baking

Preheat oven to the temperature called for in the recipe. When dough has doubled in bulk for the second time, place it in the oven and bake for required time.

To check baked goods for doneness, check to see if the loaf has begun to pull away from the sides of the pan, then remove the bread or rolls from the pan and tap the bottom. If it sounds hollow, the bread should be done. If not, return the bread to the pan and bake for a few minutes longer. Remove from pan and cool on wire racks.

Raisin Braid

3½ to 4 cups flour
1 package active dry yeast
¼ cup sugar
¼ teaspoon salt
1 cup whipping cream, lukewarm
2 eggs
1 egg white
1 teaspoon vanilla
1½ cups raisins
1 egg yolk
2 tablespoons milk

Grease a 10 x 15-inch cookie sheet.

Sift flour into a large bowl. Sprinkle yeast directly from the package onto the flour; mix together. Blend in sugar, salt, cream, eggs, egg white, and vanilla. Combine the ingredients using a wooden spoon or dough hook of an electric mixer. If using mixer, begin on the lowest setting to blend, and then adjust to high for 5 minutes. Should the dough become sticky, add a little more flour, but not too much as the dough must remain moderately soft. Place dough on a lightly floured board and knead until smooth.

Place dough in a greased bowl; turn once to grease lightly. Cover bowl with a dish towel; place in a warm, draft-free area for 1½ hours or until doubled in bulk.

Punch dough down. Turn out onto lightly floured board and knead in raisins. Shape ⅔ the dough into 3 rolls, each about 12 inches long. Braid the rolls together; place on prepared cookie sheet. Beat the egg yolk and milk together in a small bowl. Press a hollow along the length of the braid with a rolling pin. Brush the hollow with the egg yolk mixture.

From the remaining dough, form 3 rolls, each about 10 inches long; braid them together. Place this braid atop the hollow of the larger braid; brush with egg yolk mixture. Place in a warm draft-free area for 45 minutes or until doubled in bulk. Preheat oven to 375°.

Bake for 35 minutes or until golden brown and bottom sounds hollow when tapped. Remove from pan and cool on wire rack.

Makes 1 braid

Peach Cheese Cake

3 cups flour
1 package active dry yeast
⅓ cup sugar
¼ teaspoon salt
¾ cup whipping cream, lukewarm
¼ cup butter *or* margarine, melted and cooled to lukewarm
1 egg
 Peach Filling
1 tablespoon butter *or* margarine, melted
1 tablespoon sugar

Grease a 9-inch springform pan.

Sift flour into a large bowl. Sprinkle yeast directly from the package onto the flour; mix together. Blend in ⅓ cup sugar, salt, cream, lukewarm butter, and egg. Combine the ingredients using a wooden spoon or the dough hook of an electric mixer. If using a mixer, begin on the lowest setting to blend and then adjust to high for 5 minutes. Should the dough become sticky, add a little more flour, but not too much as the dough must remain moderately soft. Place dough on a lightly floured board and knead until smooth.

Place dough in a greased bowl; turn once to grease lightly. Cover bowl with a dish towel; place in a warm, draft-free area for 1½ hours or until doubled in bulk. Prepare Peach Filling while dough rises.

Punch dough down. Turn out onto lightly floured board and knead until smooth. Pat ½ the dough into the bottom and ⅔ the way up the sides of the prepared springform pan. Spread the Peach Filling evenly over the dough to within ½ inch of the top of the dough. Fold the edges of the dough over the filling.

Roll out the remaining dough on a lightly floured board to form a top crust; place this over the filling, pressing the edges together to seal. Cover; place in a warm, draft-free area for 45 minutes or until doubled in bulk.

Bake for 25 minutes or until golden brown. Immediately after baking, brush with melted butter and sprinkle with sugar. Remove from pan and cool on wire rack.

Makes 8 to 10 servings

Peach Filling

2 cups diced peaches,
  stewed *or* canned, juice
  drained and reserved
3 8-ounce packages cream
  cheese, softened
⅓ cup sugar
6 tablespoons peach juice
1 egg yolk
1 teaspoon vanilla
1 egg white, stiffly beaten

Combine peaches and cream cheese in a large bowl. Blend in sugar, peach juice, egg yolk, and vanilla. Beat until fluffy. Fold in beaten egg white; set aside.

Almond Bread

3½ to 4 cups flour
1 package active dry yeast
⅓ cup sugar
¼ teaspoon salt
1 cup whipping cream,
  lukewarm
⅓ cup butter *or* margarine,
  melted and cooled to
  lukewarm
1 egg
1 teaspoon vanilla
1 cup raisins
1 cup almonds

Grease a 9 x 5 x 3-inch loaf pan.

Sift flour into a large bowl. Sprinkle yeast directly from the package onto the flour; mix together. Blend in sugar, salt, cream, butter, egg, and vanilla. Combine the ingredients using a wooden spoon or the dough hook of an electric mixer. If using a mixer, begin on the lowest setting to blend and then adjust to high for 5 minutes. Should the dough become sticky, add a little more flour, but not too much as the dough must remain moderately soft. Place dough on a lightly floured board and knead until smooth.

Place dough in a greased bowl; turn once to grease lightly. Cover bowl with a dish towel; place in a warm, draft-free area for 1½ hours or until doubled in bulk.

Punch dough down. Turn out onto lightly floured board and knead until smooth. Knead in raisins and almonds. Shape dough into a pan-sized loaf; place loaf in prepared pan and cover lightly with towel. Place in a warm, draft-free area for 45 minutes or until doubled in bulk. Preheat oven to 375°.

Brush loaf with water and bake for 35 minutes or until golden brown and bottom sounds hollow when tapped. Brush with water immediately after baking. Remove from pan and cool on wire rack.

Makes 1 loaf

Babas au Rhum

1 package active dry yeast
1 teaspoon sugar
¼ cup lukewarm water
¼ cup milk, scalded and
   cooled to lukewarm
6 tablespoons butter,
   melted and cooled to
   lukewarm
¼ teaspoon salt
¼ cup sugar
3 eggs
2 cups flour
½ cup cake flour
   Rum Syrup
   Apricot Glaze

Butter 6 baba molds (available in gourmet stores), or use custard cups.

Sprinkle yeast and sugar over the lukewarm water; set aside for 10 minutes to dissolve. Combine milk, butter, and salt in a bowl; set aside. Combine sugar and eggs in a large bowl; beat until fluffy. Gradually add in flours, yeast mixture, and milk mixture alternately; beat until well blended. Fill prepared molds half-full with batter. Cover with buttered aluminum foil and place in a warm, draft-free area for 20 to 25 minutes or until batter rises to the top of the molds. Preheat oven to 350°.

Place molds on a cookie sheet. Bake for 15 to 20 minutes or until golden brown. Turn babas out of molds; place on wire rack to cool.

Prepare Rum Syrup. Place the rack over a cookie sheet. Slowly drizzle syrup over babas; set aside until syrup is absorbed. Prepare Apricot Glaze. Spoon warm glaze over babas. Chill until ready to serve.

Makes 6 servings

Rum Syrup

3 cups water
1½ cups sugar
⅓ cup dark rum

Heat water and sugar in a small saucepan, stirring continuously for about 5 minutes or until syrup is clear. Remove from heat. Stir in rum.

Apricot Glaze

1 cup apricot jam
2 tablespoons sugar
3 tablespoons dark rum

Combine jam and sugar in a small saucepan. Cook over medium heat until mixture boils. Stir in rum.

Almond Stollen

2 cups raisins
⅓ cup dark rum
¾ cup milk, lukewarm
1 package active dry yeast
1 tablespoon sugar
3 cups flour
⅓ cup sugar
¼ teaspoon salt
⅛ teaspoon each, ground cardamom, cloves, and mace
½ cup butter *or* margarine at room temperature
1 egg
1 teaspoon vanilla
1 cup dried currants, soaked and drained
½ cup diced candied lemon peel
½ cup chopped almonds
2 cups almond paste (available at gourmet stores)
⅓ cup butter *or* margarine, melted
½ cup confectioners' sugar

Line a 10 x 15-inch cookie sheet with parchment paper.

Place raisins and rum in a small saucepan; heat until warmed through, stirring to coat raisins. Set aside.

Pour lukewarm milk into a small bowl; add yeast and 1 tablespoon sugar, stirring until dissolved. Set aside in a warm area for 10 minutes.

Sift flour into a large bowl. Make a hollow in the center. Add ⅓ cup sugar, salt, spices, ½ cup butter, egg, and vanilla around the edges of the flour. Place the yeast liquid in the hollow, and combine ingredients using a wooden spoon or the dough hook of an electric mixer. If using mixer, begin on the lowest setting to blend and then adjust to high for 5 minutes. Should the dough become sticky, add a little more flour, but not too much as the dough must remain moderately soft. Place dough on a lightly floured board and knead until smooth.

Place dough in a greased bowl; turn once to grease lightly. Cover bowl with dish towel; place in a warm, draft-free area for 1½ hours or until doubled in bulk.

Punch dough down. Turn out onto a lightly floured board; knead in the raisins, currants, lemon peel, and almonds. Roll out the dough to form a 10 x 7-inch rectangle. Knead the almond paste until smooth. Roll out the almond paste to an 8 x 5-inch rectangle. Center the almond paste rectangle on top of the dough. Roll up dough, beginning on a long side.

Place stollen on prepared cookie sheet. Cover loosely with a dish towel and place in a warm, draft-free area for 50 minutes or until doubled in bulk.

Preheat oven to 350°.

Bake for 45 to 50 minutes or until golden brown and bottom sounds hollow when tapped. Brush stollen with melted butter and sprinkle with confectioners' sugar immediately after baking. Remove from pan and cool on wire rack.

Makes 8 to 10 servings

Almond Squares

3½ to 4 cups flour
1 package active dry yeast
⅔ cup sugar, divided
¼ teaspoon salt
1 cup milk, lukewarm
¾ cup butter *or* margarine, melted and cooled to lukewarm
2 teaspoons vanilla, divided
½ cup flaked almonds
Sugar

Grease a 10 x 15-inch cookie sheet.

Sift flour into a large bowl. Sprinkle yeast directly from package onto the flour; mix together. Blend in ⅓ cup sugar, salt, milk, ¼ cup butter, and 1 teaspoon vanilla. Combine the ingredients using a wooden spoon or the dough hook of an electric mixer. If using mixer, begin on the lowest setting to blend and then adjust to high for 5 minutes. Should the dough become sticky, add a little more flour, but not too much as the dough must remain moderately soft. Place dough on a lightly floured board and knead until smooth.

Place dough in a greased bowl; turn once to grease lightly. Cover bowl with a dish towel; place in a warm, draft-free area for 1½ hours or until doubled in bulk.

Punch dough down. Turn out onto a lightly floured board and knead until smooth. Roll out dough to fit cookie sheet. Place on prepared cookie sheet.

Brush remaining butter over dough. Combine remaining sugar and vanilla; sprinkle over dough. Spread almonds evenly over dough. Place in a warm, draft-free area for 45 minutes or until doubled in bulk. Preheat oven to 375°.

Bake for 35 minutes or until golden brown. Sprinkle with sugar. Remove from pan and cool on wire rack. Cut into squares before serving.

Makes approximately 30 squares

Braided Fruit Bread

3½ to 4 cups flour
1 package active dry yeast
⅓ cup sugar
¼ teaspoon salt
¾ cup sour cream at room temperature
½ cup milk, lukewarm
⅓ cup margarine, melted and cooled to lukewarm
1 teaspoon vanilla
4 slices canned pineapple, diced
1 cup raisins
½ cup flaked almonds

Grease a 10 x 15-inch cookie sheet.

Sift flour into a large bowl. Sprinkle yeast directly from the package onto the flour; mix together. Blend in sugar, salt, sour cream, milk, margarine, and vanilla. Combine the ingredients using a wooden spoon or the dough hook of an electric mixer. If using mixer, begin on the lowest setting to blend and then adjust to high for 5 minutes. Should the dough become sticky, add a little more flour, but not too much as the dough must remain moderately soft. Place dough on lightly floured board and knead until smooth.

Place dough in a greased bowl; turn once to grease lightly. Cover bowl with a dish towel; place in a warm, draft-free area for 1½ hours or until doubled in bulk.

Punch dough down. Divide dough into 3 equal pieces. Knead the pineapple into one of the pieces, adding more flour only if needed. Knead the raisins into a second piece, and the almonds into the remaining piece.

Shape each piece of dough into a 14-inch long roll. Braid the rolls together and place on prepared cookie sheet. Place in a warm, draft-free area for 45 minutes or until doubled in bulk. Preheat oven to 375°.

Brush the braid with water and bake for 35 minutes or until golden brown and bottom sounds hollow when tapped. Brush bread with water immediately after baking; remove from pan and cool on wire rack.

Makes 1 braid

Savory Bread Rolls

1 package active dry yeast
1 teaspoon sugar
1 cup lukewarm water
3 to 3½ cups wheat flour
1 teaspoon salt
⅛ teaspoon ground pepper
3 tablespoons vegetable oil
2 tablespoons chopped
parsley
2 tablespoons chopped
chives
1 teaspoon chopped dill
1 egg yolk
1 teaspoon water

Grease a 10 x 15-inch cookie sheet.

Sprinkle yeast and sugar in lukewarm water. Let stand in draft-free area for 5 minutes. Sift flour into a large bowl; add salt and pepper. Pour in yeast mixture; stir in oil. Combine the ingredients using a wooden spoon or the dough hook of an electric mixer. If using mixer, begin on the lowest speed to blend and then adjust to high for 5 minutes. Should the dough become sticky, add a little more flour, but not too much as the dough must remain moderately soft. Place dough on a lightly floured board and knead until smooth.

Place dough in a greased bowl; turn once to grease lightly. Cover bowl with a dish towel; place in a warm, draft-free area for 45 minutes or until doubled in bulk.

Punch dough down. Knead in herbs until smooth. Shape dough into 12 equal-sized rolls. Place on cookie sheet. Place bread in a warm, draft-free area for about 45 minutes or until doubled in bulk.

Combine egg yolk and water. Brush tops of rolls with mixture. Cut two ¼-inch deep slashes in the top of each roll, forming a cross.

Bake for 25 minutes or until rolls are golden brown and sound hollow when tapped. Remove from pan and cool on wire rack.

Makes 12 rolls

Sesame Bread

1 package active dry yeast
1 teaspoon sugar
1 cup lukewarm water
3 to 3½ cups wheat flour
1 teaspoon salt
3 tablespoons roasted
    sesame seeds
    Milk
    Sesame seeds

Grease a 9 x 5 x 3-inch loaf pan.

Sprinkle yeast and sugar in lukewarm water. Set aside in draft-free area for 5 minutes. Sift flour into a large bowl; add salt. Pour yeast mixture over flour. Combine ingredients using a wooden spoon or the dough hook of an electric mixer. If using mixer, begin on the lowest speed to blend and then adjust to high for 5 minutes. Should the dough become sticky, add a little more flour, but not too much as the dough must remain moderately soft. Place dough on a lightly floured board and knead in roasted sesame seeds until smooth.

Place dough in a greased bowl; turn once to grease lightly. Cover bowl with a dish towel; place in a warm, draft-free area for 1½ hours or until doubled in bulk.

Punch dough down and knead on pastry board until smooth, about 5 minutes; shape into a loaf. Place in loaf pan; cover and leave in a warm area for 45 minutes or until doubled in bulk. Preheat oven to 375°. Brush with milk and sprinkle with sesame seeds.

Bake for 45 minutes or until bread sounds hollow when lightly tapped on bottom. Remove from pan and cool on wire rack.

Makes 1 loaf

Party Pizzas

3½ to 4 cups flour
1 package active dry yeast
1 teaspoon sugar
¼ teaspoon salt
⅛ teaspoon ground black
    pepper
⅛ teaspoon paprika
½ cup milk, lukewarm
⅓ cup butter *or* margarine,
    melted and cooled to
    lukewarm

Grease two 10 x 15-inch cookie sheets.

Sift flour into a large bowl. Sprinkle yeast directly from the package onto the flour; mix together. Add next 7 ingredients. Combine the ingredients using a wooden spoon or the dough hook of an electric mixer. If using mixer, begin on the lowest setting to blend and then adjust to high for 5 minutes. Should the dough become sticky, add a little more flour, but not too much as the dough must remain moderately soft. Place dough on a lightly floured board and knead until smooth.

2 eggs
4 medium tomatoes, peeled and chopped
1 cup sautéed mushrooms
½ pound salami *or* pepperoni, thinly sliced
2 medium onions, thinly sliced and sautéed
   Oregano to taste
2 cups grated mozzarella cheese

Place dough in a greased bowl; turn once to grease lightly. Cover bowl with dish towel; place in a warm, draft-free area for 1½ hours or until doubled in bulk.

Punch dough down. Turn out onto lightly floured board and knead until smooth. Divide dough into 8 equal pieces. Form each piece of dough into a 4-inch circle. Place circles on prepared cookie sheets. Divide remaining ingredients equally among the circles.

Bake for 20 to 25 minutes or until dough is lightly browned and cheese is melted. Serve hot.

Makes 8 servings

Yeast Pound Cake

¾ cup whipping cream, lukewarm
1 package active dry yeast
2 teaspoons sugar
3½ cups flour
¾ cup sugar
¾ cup ground almonds
   Zest of ½ lemon
¾ cup butter *or* margarine, melted and cooled to lukewarm
3 eggs
1 teaspoon vanilla
1½ cups raisins
3 tablespoons slivered almonds
   Confectioners' sugar

Grease a bundt pan or an 8-inch turban pan.

Pour whipping cream into a small bowl. Stir in yeast and 2 teaspoons sugar; set aside for 5 minutes. Sift flour into a large bowl. Make a hollow in the center. Add ¾ cup sugar, ground almonds, lemon zest, cooled butter, eggs, and vanilla around the edges of the flour. Pour yeast liquid into the hollow. Combine the ingredients using a wooden spoon or the dough hook of an electric mixer. If using mixer, begin on the lowest setting and then adjust to high for 5 minutes. Should the dough become sticky, add a little more flour, but not too much as the dough must remain moderately soft. Place dough on a lightly floured board; knead in raisins.

Sprinkle slivered almonds in the bottom of the prepared pan. Use rubber spatula to spread dough evenly in pan. Place in a warm, draft-free area for 2½ hours or until doubled in bulk. Preheat oven to 350°.

Bake for 40 to 45 minutes or until a wooden skewer inserted in center comes out clean. Turn out cake onto wire rack to cool; dust generously with confectioners' sugar.

Makes 10 to 12 servings

Apple Streusel Cake

1 cup milk, lukewarm
1 package active dry yeast
2 teaspoons sugar
3½ to 4 cups flour
¼ cup sugar
¼ teaspoon salt
¼ cup butter *or* margarine, melted and cooled to lukewarm
1 teaspoon vanilla
3½ cups peeled, thinly sliced cooking apples
½ cup slivered almonds
½ cup golden raisins
1 teaspoon cinnamon
⅛ cup sugar

Grease a 9 x 13-inch cake pan.

Pour lukewarm milk into a small bowl. Add yeast and sugar, stirring until dissolved. Set aside in warm area for 5 minutes. Sift flour into a large bowl. Make a hollow in the center. Add ¼ cup sugar, salt, butter, and vanilla around edges of the flour. Pour the yeast liquid into the hollow. Combine the ingredients using a wooden spoon or the dough hook of an electric mixer. If using mixer, begin on the lowest speed to blend and then adjust to high for 5 minutes. Should the dough become sticky, add a little more flour, but not too much as the dough must remain moderately soft. Place dough on a lightly floured board and knead until smooth.

Place dough in a greased bowl; turn once to grease lightly. Cover bowl with a dish towel; place in a warm, draft-free area for 45 minutes or until doubled in bulk.

Punch dough down. Pat dough into prepared pan. Arrange apple slices on top of dough.

Place dough in a warm, draft-free area for 45 minutes or until doubled in bulk. Preheat oven to 375°. Sprinkle dough with almonds, raisins, cinnamon and sugar.

Bake on center rack of oven for 25 to 30 minutes or until golden brown. Remove from pan; cool on wire rack. To serve, cut into 2 x 3-inch strips.

Makes approximately 18

Poppy Seed Roll

¾ cup milk, lukewarm
1 package active dry yeast
1 teaspoon sugar
3 to 3½ cups flour
¼ teaspoon salt
¾ cup butter *or* margarine,
  melted and cooled to
  lukewarm, divided
1 egg
1 teaspoon vanilla
2 cups ground poppy seed
¼ cup ground almonds
1 cup candied lemon peel,
  diced
¾ cup raisins
  Milk
  Lemon Icing
  Flaked almonds

Grease a 10 x 15-inch cookie sheet.

Pour lukewarm milk into a small bowl. Stir in yeast and sugar; set aside for 5 minutes. Sift flour into a large bowl. Make a hollow in the center. Add salt, ¼ cup melted butter, egg, and vanilla around the edges of the flour. Pour the yeast liquid into the hollow. Combine the ingredients using a wooden spoon or the dough hook of an electric mixer. If using mixer, begin on the lowest setting to blend and then adjust to high for 5 minutes. Should the dough become sticky, add a little more flour, but not too much as the dough must remain moderately soft. Place dough on a lightly floured board and knead until smooth.

Place dough in a greased bowl; turn once to grease lightly. Cover bowl with a dish towel; place in a warm, draft-free area for 1½ hours or until doubled in bulk.

Combine remaining butter, poppy seed, ground almonds, lemon peel, and raisins in large bowl. Set aside.

Punch dough down. Turn out onto a lightly floured board and knead until smooth. Roll out dough to form a 10 x 12-inch rectangle. Spread poppy seed mixture evenly over dough to within ½ inch of the edges.

Fold the clean edges of the shorter side over the filling. Roll up dough jelly-roll style, beginning on a long side. Place dough on prepared cookie sheet. Cover with a dish towel; place in a warm, draft-free area for 45 minutes or until doubled in bulk. Preheat oven to 350°.

Cut a ¼-inch deep slash along length of roll. Brush with milk. Bake for 40 minutes or until a skewer inserted in center comes out clean. Prepare Lemon Icing while roll bakes.

Spread icing over poppy seed roll as soon as it is removed from the oven. Sprinkle with flaked almonds. Place on wire rack to cool. Cut into slices before serving.

Makes 10 to 12 servings

Lemon Icing

¾ cup confectioners' sugar,
   sifted
3 tablespoons lemon juice

Combine sugar and lemon juice in a small bowl until smooth.

Cheese Bread

1 package active dry yeast
1 teaspoon sugar
1 cup lukewarm water
3 to 3½ cups wheat flour
1 teaspoon salt
⅛ teaspoon ground black
   pepper
3 tablespoons vegetable oil
¾ cup Emmenthaler cheese,
   cut into small cubes
⅓ cup Emmenthaler cheese,
   cut into wedges
1 egg yolk
1 tablespoon water

Grease an 8-inch soufflé dish.

Sprinkle yeast and sugar in ½ cup of the luke-warm water. Set aside in a warm area for 5 minutes. Sift flour into a large bowl; add salt and pepper. Pour yeast mixture over flour. Stir in remaining water and oil. Combine ingredients using a wooden spoon or the dough hook of an electric mixer. If using mixer, begin on the lowest speed to blend and then adjust to high for 5 minutes. Should the dough become sticky, add a little more flour, but not too much as the dough must remain moderately soft. Place dough on a lightly floured board and knead until smooth.

Place dough in a greased bowl; turn once to grease lightly. Cover bowl with a dish towel; place in a warm, draft-free area for 1½ hours or until doubled in bulk.

Punch dough down. Place on pastry board and knead in the cubes of cheese until dough is smooth. Shape into a circle and place in the soufflé dish. Insert cheese wedges into the dough. Cover and place in a warm, draft-free area for about 45 minutes or until doubled in bulk. Preheat oven to 400°.

Mix egg yolk and water together. Brush top of bread with egg glaze.

Bake for 50 minutes or until bottom sounds hollow when tapped. Remove the bread from dish; cool on wire rack.

Makes 1 loaf

Almond Custard Slices

½ cup milk, lukewarm
1 package active dry yeast
1 teaspoon sugar
3½ to 4 cups flour
⅓ cup sugar
¼ teaspoon salt
¼ cup butter *or* margarine,
  melted and cooled to
  lukewarm
2 eggs
1 teaspoon vanilla
  Almond Topping
  Custard Filling

Grease a 10 x 15-inch jelly-roll pan.

Pour lukewarm milk into a small bowl. Stir in yeast and 1 teaspoon sugar; set aside for 5 minutes. Sift flour into a large bowl. Make a hollow in the center. Add ⅓ cup sugar, salt, cooled butter, eggs, and vanilla around the edges of the flour. Pour the yeast liquid into the hollow. Combine the ingredients using a wooden spoon or the dough hook of an electric mixer. If using mixer, begin on the lowest setting to blend and then adjust to high for 5 minutes. Should the dough become sticky, add a little more flour, but not too much as the dough must remain moderately soft. Place dough on a lightly floured board and knead until smooth.

Place dough in a greased bowl; turn once to grease lightly. Cover bowl with a dish towel; place in a warm, draft-free area for 45 minutes or until doubled in bulk. Prepare Almond Topping.

Punch dough down. Turn out onto a floured board and knead until smooth. Roll out dough to fit or pat into prepared pan. Prick several times with a fork.

Spread Almond Topping evenly over dough. Cover lightly and place in a warm, draft-free area for 45 minutes or until doubled in bulk. Preheat oven to 375°.

Bake for 15 minutes or until a wooden skewer inserted in center comes out clean. Set aside to cool on wire rack for 15 to 20 minutes. Prepare Custard Filling while cake is baking.

Cut cooled cake into quarters. Slice each quarter in half horizontally. Spread the bottom half of each quarter with Custard Filling. Cover with top layers. Slice each quarter into serving pieces.

Makes 10 to 12 servings

Almond Topping

¼ cup butter *or* margarine
¾ cup sugar
6 tablespoons milk
1 teaspoon vanilla
2 cups chopped almonds

Melt butter in saucepan over medium heat. Add remaining ingredients; stir until well blended. Set aside for 5 to 10 minutes.

Custard Filling

5 egg yolks
1 cup sugar
½ cup flour
2 cups milk, scalded and
   cooled to lukewarm
1 tablespoon butter *or*
   margarine
2 teaspoons vanilla
2 cups whipping cream,
   chilled

Beat egg yolks in a large bowl until light and fluffy. Sprinkle with sugar; continue beating until sugar has dissolved. Whisk in flour until well blended. Stir in milk in a slow, steady stream until combined.

Place mixture in top of double boiler over simmering water; heat until custard begins to boil, stirring contantly. Continue to heat and stir for 2 to 3 minutes. Remove pan from heat. Stir in butter and vanilla; set aside to cool.

Beat whipping cream until stiff peaks form. Fold into cooled custard; chill for 20 minutes.

Cinnamon Rounds

1 package active dry yeast
¼ cup lukewarm water
3 cups flour
¼ teaspoon salt
2 tablespoons sugar
1 cup butter *or* margarine at
   room temperature
½ cup milk, lukewarm
1 egg, slightly beaten
3 tablespoons vegetable oil
½ cup sugar
½ cup firmly packed brown
   sugar
2 tablespoons ground
   cinnamon

Sprinkle yeast over lukewarm water; set aside for 5 minutes. Combine flour, salt, and 2 tablespoons sugar in a large bowl. Cut in butter using a pastry blender, a fork, or the dough hook of an electric mixer. Blend milk, egg, and oil together in a separate bowl; stir in yeast liquid. Pour milk mixture over flour; stir with a fork just until all the ingredients are moistened. Cover and chill for 1 hour.

Turn out dough onto a lightly floured board; knead with a push-pull motion 4 or 5 times. Roll out dough to form an 11 x 18-inch rectangle. Combine sugars and cinnamon in a small bowl. Sprinkle ½ of the mixture over dough. Roll the dough up jelly-roll style, very tightly, beginning on a long side. Pinch edges together to seal. Wrap in plastic wrap; chill for 1 hour or until firm. Preheat oven to 400°.

Cut dough into ½-inch thick slices. Sprinkle both sides of each slice with remaining sugar mixture. Flatten each slice into a 5-inch circle. Sprinkle with more sugar if dough is sticky. Place dough circles on a 10 x 15-inch non-stick cookie sheet.

Bake for 10 to 12 minutes or until lightly browned. Remove from cookie sheet and place on wire rack to cool. Store in an airtight container.

Makes 10 to 12 servings

Jelly Doughnuts

½ cup milk, lukewarm
1 package active dry yeast
1 teaspoon sugar
3½ to 4 cups flour
2 tablespoons sugar
¼ teaspoon salt
¼ cup butter *or* margarine,
    melted and cooled to
    lukewarm
2 eggs
1 egg yolk
1 teaspoon vanilla
1 egg white, slightly beaten
½ cup raspberry jelly
    Vegetable oil
    Sugar

Pour lukewarm milk into a small bowl. Stir in yeast and 1 teaspoon sugar; set aside for 5 minutes. Sift flour into a large bowl. Make a hollow in the center. Add 2 tablespoons sugar, salt, butter, eggs, egg yolk, and vanilla around the edges of the flour. Pour the yeast liquid into the hollow. Combine the ingredients using a wooden spoon or the dough hook of an electric mixer. If using mixer, begin on the lowest setting to blend and then adjust to high for 5 minutes. Should the dough become sticky, add a little more flour, but not too much as the dough must remain moderately soft. Place dough on a lightly floured board and knead until smooth.

Place dough in a greased bowl; turn once to grease lightly. Cover the bowl with a dish towel; place in a warm, draft-free area for 1½ hours or until doubled in bulk.

Punch dough down. Turn out dough onto lightly floured board; knead until smooth. Roll out dough to a ¼-inch thickness. Use a cookie cutter to cut out 2½-inch diameter circles. Brush edges with egg white. Place 1½ teaspoons of jelly in the middle of half of the circles. Cover with remaining circles; press edges firmly together. Place doughnuts in a warm, draft-free area for 25 minutes or until doubled in bulk.

Use a deep fryer or pour oil into a heavy, deep skillet to a depth of 1½ inches. If using deep fryer, follow manufacturer's instructions. Heat oil to 375°. Slide doughnuts gently into hot oil. Do not crowd. Turn doughnuts after one side is browned. Remove with slotted spoon when second side is brown; drain on paper towels. Set aside to cool. Roll cooled doughnuts in sugar.

Makes 12 to 16 doughnuts

Stuffed Ring

3½ to 4 cups flour
1 package active dry yeast
½ cup sugar
¼ teaspoon salt
¾ cup milk, lukewarm
½ cup butter *or* margarine, melted and cooled to lukewarm
1 egg
3 tablespoons butter *or* margarine at room temperature
1 cup raisins
½ cup dried currants, soaked and drained
½ cup candied lemon peel
½ cup chopped almonds
¼ cup sugar
1 teaspoon vanilla
Milk
½ cup confectioners' sugar
2 tablespoons hot water

Grease a 10x15-inch cookie sheet.

Sift flour into a large mixing bowl. Sprinkle yeast directly from the package onto the flour; mix together. Blend in ½ cup sugar, salt, milk, ½ cup butter, and egg. Combine the ingredients using a wooden spoon or the dough hook of an electric mixer. If using mixer, begin on the lowest setting to blend and then adjust to high for 5 minutes. Should the dough become sticky, add a little more flour, but not too much as the dough must remain moderately soft. Place dough on a lightly floured board; knead until smooth.

Place dough in a greased bowl; turn once to grease lightly. Cover dough with a dish towel and place in a warm, draft-free area for 1½ hours or until doubled in bulk.

Punch dough down. Turn out onto a lightly floured board; roll out to form a 10 x 12-inch rectangle. Spread dough with room temperature butter and cut dough in ½ lengthwise.

Toss raisins, currants, lemon peel, almonds, ¼ cup sugar, and vanilla together in a large bowl. Spread fruit mixture over each half of dough, leaving a ½-inch clean edge on all sides.

Roll up each half of dough, jelly-roll style, beginning on a long side. Twist each roll; pinch ends together. Place rolls on cookie sheet to form a ring.

Using a pair of kitchen scissors or sharp knife, make a ½-inch deep cut into the outer edges of the ring every 2 to 3 inches all around the dough. Brush with milk. Cover with a sheet of buttered aluminum foil; set aside in a warm, draft-free area for 45 minutes or until doubled in bulk. Preheat oven to 375°.

Bake for 25 to 35 minutes or until golden brown. Remove from pan; cool on wire rack. Blend confectioners' sugar and hot water until smooth. Drizzle over the ring.

Makes 8 to 10 servings

Rock Almond Roll

Fine bread crumbs
¾ cup milk, lukewarm
1 package active dry yeast
2 teaspoons sugar
3 to 3½ cups flour
3 tablespoons sugar
¼ teaspoon salt
¼ cup butter *or* margarine, melted and cooled to lukewarm
2 eggs
1 teaspoon vanilla
2 tablespoons butter *or* margarine, divided
2 tablespoons sugar
¾ cup chopped almonds
2 cups almond paste (available at gourmet stores)
2 tablespoons melted butter *or* margarine
2 tablespoons confectioners' sugar

Grease a 9 x 5 x 3-inch loaf pan. Sprinkle with fine bread crumbs.

Pour lukewarm milk into small bowl; add yeast and sugar, stirring until dissolved. Set aside in a warm area for 5 minutes. Sift flour into a large bowl. Make a hollow in the center. Add 3 tablespoons sugar, salt, cooled butter, 1 egg, and vanilla around the edges of the flour. Pour yeast liquid into the hollow; combine the ingredients using a wooden spoon or the dough hook of an electric mixer. If using mixer, begin on the lowest setting and then adjust to high for 5 minutes. Should the dough become sticky, add a little more flour, but not too much as the dough must remain moderately soft. Place dough on a lightly floured board and knead until smooth.

Place dough in a greased bowl; turn once to grease lightly. Cover bowl with a dish towel; place in a warm, draft-free area for 1½ hours or until doubled in bulk.

Melt 1 tablespoon butter and remaining sugar in skillet over medium heat, stirring until dissolved. Add almonds and continue stirring until almonds are golden brown. Set aside to cool.

Knead almond paste until soft and smooth. Mix in 1 tablespoon butter and remaining egg; set aside.

Punch dough down. Turn out dough onto a lightly floured board; knead until smooth. Roll out dough to form a 9 x 8-inch rectangle. Spread almond paste over dough; sprinkle with browned almonds. Roll up dough jelly-roll style, beginning on a short side. Place in prepared loaf pan. Cover lightly with towel; place in a warm, draft-free area for 45 minutes or until doubled in bulk. Preheat oven to 375°.

Cut two ½-inch deep slashes lengthwise into the top of the roll. Bake for 30 minutes or until golden brown and bottom sounds hollow when tapped. Remove from pan; place on wire rack. Brush with melted butter; sprinkle with confectioners' sugar.

Makes 8 to 10 servings

Breakfast Rolls

¾ cup milk, lukewarm
1 package active dry yeast
2 teaspoons sugar
3½ to 4 cups flour
¾ cup sugar
¼ teaspoon salt
¼ cup butter *or* margarine, melted and cooled to lukewarm
1 egg
1 teaspoon vanilla
2 tablespoons butter *or* margarine

Pour lukewarm milk into a small bowl. Stir in yeast and 2 teaspoons sugar; set aside for 5 minutes. Sift flour into a large bowl. Make a hollow in the center. Add ¾ cup sugar, salt, cooled butter, egg, and vanilla around the edges of the flour. Pour yeast liquid into the hollow. Combine ingredients using a wooden spoon or the dough hook of an electric mixer. If using mixer, begin on the lowest setting to blend and then adjust to high for 5 minutes. Should the dough become sticky, add a little more flour, but not too much as the dough must remain moderately soft. Place dough on a lightly floured board and knead until smooth.

Place dough in a greased bowl; turn once to grease lightly. Cover bowl with a dish towel; place in a warm, draft-free area for 1½ hours or until doubled in bulk.

Punch dough down. Turn out onto a lightly floured board and knead until smooth. Form dough into a long rope shape; cut into 12 equal pieces. Shape pieces into balls.

Melt 2 tablespoons butter in a 9-inch soufflé dish or pie plate.

Roll the dough balls in the melted butter; cover lightly with buttered aluminum foil and place in a warm, draft-free area for 25 minutes or until doubled in bulk. Preheat oven to 400°.

Bake for 25 to 30 minutes or until rolls are golden brown and sound hollow when bottom is tapped. Remove and cool on wire rack.

Makes 12 rolls

Apricot Cheese Crescents

¾ cup milk, lukewarm
1 package active dry yeast
2 teaspoons sugar
3 cups flour
¼ teaspoon salt
3 tablespoons butter *or* margarine, melted and cooled to lukewarm
15 apricot halves, cut into quarters
1 cup grated Emmenthaler cheese

Grease a 10 x 15-inch cookie sheet.

Pour lukewarm milk into a small bowl. Stir in yeast and sugar; set aside for 5 minutes. Sift flour into a large bowl. Make a hollow in the center. Add salt and butter around the edges of the flour. Pour yeast liquid into the hollow. Combine ingredients using a wooden spoon or the dough hook of an electric mixer. If using mixer, begin on the lowest setting to blend and then adjust to high for 5 minutes. Should the dough become sticky, add a little more flour, but not too much as the dough must remain moderately soft. Place dough on a lightly floured board and knead until smooth.

Place dough in a greased bowl; turn once to grease lightly. Cover bowl with a dish towel; place in a warm, draft-free area for 1½ hours or until doubled in bulk.

Punch dough down. Turn out onto lightly floured board; knead until smooth. Roll out dough to form a 9 x 18-inch rectangle. Cut into 3-inch squares.

Place 1 or 2 apricot pieces onto each square of dough. Roll up dough squares from 1 corner. Bend them into a crescent shape and place on prepared cookie sheet. Cover lightly and place in a warm, draft-free area for 25 minutes or until doubled in bulk. Preheat oven to 400°.

Brush crescents with water; sprinkle with cheese. Bake for 10 to 15 minutes or until golden brown. Remove from cookie sheet and cool on wire rack.

Makes 15 servings

Gift and Specialty Baking

Gift and Specialty Baking

The "Gift and Specialty Baking" chapter is divided into 2 sections: Flaky Yeast Pastry and Baking with Sour Cream. Each presents recipes for baking moist pastries, cakes, and tarts to give as gifts or to serve for family and friends.

Flaky pastry is chilled twice before baking to give the dough a resting period between each work stage. The chilling method has a distinct advantage in that you can bake the dough after the last chilling period or you can store it in the refrigerator for 2 to 3 days and bake it as needed.

The Individual Steps

1 Sift the flour into a large bowl.

2 Sprinkle with yeast and sugar.

3 Stir until mixed.

1 Add the eggs, milk, salt, flavorings, and butter pieces.

2 Stir the ingredients together to begin the mixing process.

1 Combine the ingredients using a wooden spoon or the dough hook of an electric mixer. If using an electric mixer, begin on the lowest setting to blend, then adjust mixer to high for 5 minutes to knead.

2 You can also knead by hand until smooth.

3 Set dough aside for 5 minutes after kneading.

1 Roll out dough on a lightly floured board.

2 Spread half the dough with the cut butter pieces.

3 Fold the remaining half of the dough over the butter-covered portion.

4 Press the dough halves together lightly with a rolling pin.

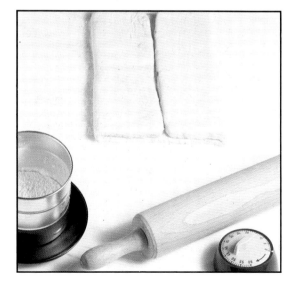

1 Roll the dough out again.

2 Fold the shorter sides over to meet in the center.

3 Fold the long sides over to create 4 layers of pastry.

4 Chill the pastry for 15 minutes.

1 Remove the dough from the refrigerator.

2 Roll out the dough to the required dimensions.

3 Fold the short sides over to meet in the center.

4 Fold the long sides over to again create 4 layers of pastry.

5 Chill for another 15 minutes.

1 Remove the dough from the refrigerator.

2 Cut, shape, or roll according to the recipe instructions.

3 Fill as instructed.

4 Set the dough aside at room temperature for 15 minutes before baking.

5 Place pastries on a lightly greased baking sheet.

6 Bake the flaky pastries at the temperature called for in the recipe for the time specified or until pastries are golden brown.

7 Remove the pastries and place on a wire rack to cool.

Flaky Yeast Ring

(Illustrated on pp. 178-179)

3½ **to 4 cups flour**
 1 **package active dry yeast**
 ¼ **cup sugar**
 ¼ **teaspoon salt**
 1 **cup milk at room temperature**

Grease a 10 x 15-inch cookie sheet.

Sift flour into a large bowl. Sprinkle with yeast and sugar; mix well. Add salt, milk, 4 tablespoons butter, egg, and vanilla. Combine the ingredients using a wooden spoon or the dough hook of an electric mixer. If using mixer, begin on the lowest setting to

4 tablespoons butter *or* margarine; cut into small pieces
1 egg
1 teaspoon vanilla
1½ cups butter *or* margarine, cut into small pieces
Almond Filling
1½ cups raisins
½ cup chopped almonds
6 tablespoons apricot jam, sieved
2 tablespoons water
½ cup confectioners' sugar
2 tablespoons dark rum
Flaked almonds

blend, then adjust to high for 5 minutes. Set dough aside for 5 minutes.

Roll out dough on a lightly floured board to form an 8 x 15-inch rectangle. Place the remaining butter pieces over half of the dough; fold the remaining half of the dough over the butter-covered portion. Press together lightly with a rolling pin.

Roll the dough out again to form an 8 x 15-inch rectangle. Fold the shorter sides over to meet in the center. Fold the long sides over to form 4 layers of pastry. Chill for 15 minutes.

Roll out dough and fold again as directed above. Chill for 15 minutes. Prepare Almond Filling.

Roll out dough to form a 12 x 17-inch rectangle. Spread Almond Filling evenly over the dough. Sprinkle with raisins and chopped almonds. Cut the dough in half lengthwise.

Roll up each half of dough beginning on a long side and twist the 2 halves together. Form into a ring on prepared cookie sheet. Set aside at room temperature for 15 minutes. Preheat oven to 375°.

Bake for 35 to 40 minutes or until golden brown. Remove from cookie sheet and place on wire rack to cool.

Combine jam and water in a small saucepan; bring to a boil, stirring constantly until blended. Spread on ring; set aside to cool.

Combine sugar and rum in a small bowl until smooth. Drizzle over cooled ring. Sprinkle with flaked almonds.

Makes 8 to 10 servings

Almond Filling

2 cups almond paste (available at gourmet stores)
3 tablespoons butter *or* margarine at room temperature
2 tablespoons dark rum

Cream almond paste with butter in a bowl until smooth. Stir in rum until well blended.

Colorful Flaky Pastries

3½ to 4 cups flour
1 package active dry yeast
¼ cup sugar
¼ teaspoon salt
1 cup milk at room temperature
4 tablespoons butter *or* margarine, cut into small pieces
1 egg
1 teaspoon vanilla
1½ cups butter *or* margarine, cut into small pieces
Peaches, canned in their own juices, cut into 1-inch pieces, juice reserved
Maraschino cherries
Peach Icing

Grease a 10 x 15-inch cookie sheet.

Sift flour into a large bowl. Sprinkle with yeast and sugar; mix well. Add salt, milk, 4 tablespoons butter, egg, and vanilla. Combine the ingredients using a wooden spoon or the dough hook of an electric mixer. If using mixer, begin on the lowest setting to blend, then adjust to high for 5 minutes. Set dough aside for 5 minutes.

Roll out dough on a lightly floured board to form an 8 x 15-inch rectangle. Place the remaining butter pieces over half of the dough; fold the remaining half of the dough over the butter-covered portion. Press together lightly with a rolling pin.

Roll the dough out again to form an 8 x 15-inch rectangle. Fold the shorter sides over to meet in the center. Fold the long sides over to form 4 layers of pastry. Chill for 15 minutes.

Roll out dough and fold again as directed above. Chill for 15 minutes.

Roll out dough to form a 6 x 16-inch rectangle. Cut into 3-inch squares. Place squares on prepared cookie sheet.

Top each square with a peach slice and a cherry. Fold pastries into triangles and press edges together. Set aside at room temperature for 15 minutes. Preheat oven to 375°.

Bake for 15 minutes or until golden brown. Remove from pan and cool on wire rack. Prepare Peach Icing and drizzle over pastries.

Makes 10 servings

Peach Icing

1 cup confectioners' sugar, sifted
2 to 4 tablespoons peach juice

Combine sugar and juice in small bowl until smooth and spreadable.

— *Flaky Hazelnut Slices* —

3½ to 4 cups flour
1 package active dry yeast
¼ cup sugar
¼ teaspoon salt
1 cup milk at room
   temperature
4 tablespoons butter *or*
   margarine, cut into small
   pieces
1 egg
1 teaspoon vanilla
1½ cups butter *or* margarine,
   cut into small pieces
   Hazelnut Filling
½ cup raisins, soaked in ⅛
   cup rum
1 egg yolk
3 tablespoons milk
¾ cup confectioners' sugar
2 to 4 tablespoons water

Grease a 10 x 15-inch cookie sheet.

Sift flour into a large bowl. Sprinkle with yeast and sugar; mix well. Add salt, 1 cup milk, 4 table-spoons butter, egg, and vanilla. Combine the ingredients using a wooden spoon or the dough hook of an electric mixer. If using mixer, begin on the lowest setting to blend, then adjust to high for 5 minutes. Set dough aside for 5 minutes.

Roll out dough on a lightly floured board to form an 8 x 15-inch rectangle. Place the remaining butter pieces over half of the dough; fold the remaining half of the dough over the butter-covered portion. Press together lightly with a rolling pin.

Roll the dough out again to form an 8 x 15-inch rectangle. Fold the shorter sides over to meet in the center. Fold the long sides over to form 4 layers of pastry. Chill for 15 minutes.

Roll out dough and fold again as directed above. Chill for 15 minutes. Prepare Hazelnut Filling.

Roll out dough to form a 12 x 15-inch rectangle. Spread with Hazelnut Filling; sprinkle with raisins.

Roll up the dough, beginning on a long side; cut in half lengthwise. Twist the 2 halves together; place on prepared cookie sheet.

Beat egg yolk and milk together in a small bowl; brush over dough. Set aside at room temperature for 15 minutes. Preheat oven to 375°.

Bake for 35 to 45 minutes or until golden brown. Remove from cookie sheet after baking and place on wire rack to cool.

Blend sugar and enough water in a small bowl to make a smooth glaze. Cut cooled pastry into slices. Drizzle glaze over slices.

Makes 8 to 10 servings

———— *Hazelnut Filling* ————

2 cups ground hazelnuts
½ cup sugar
1 egg
1 egg white
1 teaspoon vanilla

Combine all ingredients in a small bowl; stir until well blended.

— *Marzipan Flaky Pastries* —

3½ to 4 cups flour
1 package active dry yeast
¼ cup sugar
¼ teaspoon salt
1 cup milk at room
   temperature
4 tablespoons butter *or*
   margarine, cut into small
   pieces
1 egg
1 teaspoon vanilla
1½ cups butter *or* margarine,
   cut into small pieces
   Marzipan Filling
1 cup confectioners' sugar
2 to 4 tablespoons orange
   juice

Grease a 10 x 15-inch cookie sheet.

Sift flour into a large bowl. Sprinkle with yeast and sugar. Add salt, milk, 4 tablespoons butter, egg, and vanilla. Combine the ingredients using a wooden spoon or the dough hook of an electric mixer. If using mixer, begin on the lowest setting to blend, then adjust to high for 5 minutes. Set dough aside for 5 minutes.

Roll out dough on a lightly floured board to form an 8 x 15-inch rectangle. Place the remaining butter pieces over half the dough; fold the remaining half of the dough over the butter-covered portion. Press together lightly with a rolling pin.

Roll the dough out again to form an 8 x 15-inch rectangle. Fold the shorter sides over to meet in the center. Fold the long sides over to form 4 layers of pastry. Chill for 15 minutes.

Roll out dough and fold again as directed above. Chill for 15 minutes. Prepare Marzipan Filling.

Roll out dough to form a 12 x 15-inch rectangle. Spread the Marzipan Filling over half of the dough. Fold the remaining half of the dough over the filled half. Press lightly with a rolling pin.

Cut the dough in half lengthwise, then cut each half into 1-inch wide strips. Cut a 2-inch long slash in the center of each strip.

Place pastries on prepared cookie sheet; pull the sides of each strip somewhat apart. Set aside for 15 minutes. Preheat oven to 400°.

Bake for 15 minutes or until golden brown.

Combine sugar and orange juice in a small bowl until smooth.

Remove pastries from oven; place on wire rack. Drizzle with icing.

Makes approximately 15 pastries

—— *Marzipan Filling* ——

1½ cups almond paste
½ cup ground almonds
1 egg
2 tablespoons orange liqueur

Combine all ingredients in a bowl until smooth and spreadable.

Gift and Specialty Baking

Baking cakes or pastries with sour cream gives an added richness to the dough or batter. Sour cream combined with the oil in each recipe gives a smooth and tender texture to the finished baked goods. These recipes use dairy sour cream, not homemade soured cream. Be sure the sour cream is fresh before using. *Do not* substitute sour half-and-half for sour cream in these recipes.

The Individual Steps

1 Sift the flour and baking powder together into a large bowl.

2 Stir in the ingredients in the order listed in the recipe.

3 Always check the eggs for freshness by first breaking into a cup.

4 **Do not** replace the vegetable oil called for in the recipe with solid shortening.

1 Combine the ingredients using a wooden spoon or the dough hook of an electric mixer. If using an electric mixer, combine ingredients using highest setting for 1 minute.

2 Turn out dough onto a lightly floured board.

3 Shape into a roll.

4 If the dough is too soft, add a little more flour, but not too much as the dough must remain moderately soft.

1. Roll, shape, cut, or use the dough as called for in the recipe.

2. To make the small pinwheel pastries illustrated here, roll the dough out to a ¼-inch thickness.

3. Cut into squares using a pastry wheel or pastry cutter.

Baking

Bake all sour cream dough according to recipe instructions. The pastries or cakes should be removed from the baking pan as soon as it is removed from the oven. Place on wire rack to cool. The sour cream dough cakes and pastries are best when served within a day or two of being baked.

Apricot Crescents

1 cup butter *or* margarine at room temperature
2 cups flour
1 cup sour cream
1 egg, slightly beaten
½ cup apricot preserves
½ cup finely chopped walnuts
Confectioners' sugar

Cut butter into flour in bowl with pastry blender or fork until coarse crumbs form. Stir in sour cream and egg until dough holds together. Divide dough into thirds; form each third into a ball and cover with plastic wrap. Chill 3 hours or overnight.

Preheat oven to 375°. Roll out dough ⅓ at a time on lightly floured board to form an 11-inch circle. Spread with ⅓ of the preserves; sprinkle with ⅓ of the nuts.

Cut dough into 12 triangles with sharp knife. Roll each triangle starting at wide end to opposite point; form into crescent. Place, pointed-seam-side down, on 10 x 15-inch cookie sheet. Repeat with remaining dough, preserves, and nuts.

Bake for 20 minutes or until golden. Remove from pan and cool on wire rack. Sprinkle with confectioners' sugar.

Makes approximately 3 dozen

Fruit Slices

(Illustrated on pp. 188-189)

3 cups flour
2 teaspoons baking powder
¾ cup sugar, divided
¼ teaspoon salt
1 cup sour cream
6 tablespoons milk
½ cup vegetable oil
1 egg
1 teaspoon vanilla
4 tablespoons butter *or*
  margarine, melted and
  cooled to lukewarm
1 cup chopped almonds
¾ cup raisins
¾ cup currants
2 tablespoons orange juice

Preheat oven to 375°. Grease a 9-inch round cake pan or pie pan.

Sift flour and baking powder into a large bowl; stir in ½ cup sugar, salt, sour cream, milk, oil, egg, and vanilla. Combine the ingredients using a wooden spoon or the dough hook of an electric mixer. If using mixer, combine the ingredients using the highest setting for 1 minute.

Shape dough into a roll on a lightly floured board. Dough will be soft. Roll out dough to a 12 x 17-inch rectangle. Brush with melted butter.

Combine all remaining ingredients in a large bowl. Spread fruit mixture over dough. Roll up dough jelly-roll style, beginning on a long side. Slice the roll into 10 equal pieces; place slices in prepared pan. Brush slices with remaining butter.

Bake for 40 minutes or until golden brown. Remove from pan and place on wire rack to cool.

Makes 10 servings

Raisin Cake Squares

2½ cups flour
1 tablespoon baking
  powder
1½ cups sugar, divided
¼ teaspoon salt
3 cups sour cream, divided
¼ cup milk
¼ cup vegetable oil
3 eggs
2 teaspoons vanilla,
  divided
½ cup raisins
4 tablespoons milk
2 tablespoons butter *or*
  margarine, melted, and
  cooled to lukewarm

Preheat oven to 375°. Grease a 9 x 13-inch baking pan.

Sift flour and baking powder into a large bowl; stir in 1 cup sugar, salt, 1 cup sour cream, milk, oil, 2 eggs, and 1 teaspoon vanilla. Combine the ingredients using a wooden spoon or the dough hook of an electric mixer. If using mixer, combine ingredients using highest setting for 1 minute. Spread batter in prepared pan; cover with foil and set aside.

Combine remaining ingredients in a large bowl until well blended; spread evenly over batter. Bake for 35 minutes or until a wooden skewer inserted in center comes out clean. Place pan on wire rack to cool; cut into 2-inch squares.

Makes approximately 24 squares

Cherry Crescents

¾ cup butter *or* margarine,
   chilled and cut into small
   pieces
1 3-ounce package cream
   cheese
2 cups flour
1 egg, separated
¾ cup sour cream
⅔ cup cherry preserves
   Confectioners' sugar

Cut butter and cream cheese into flour in bowl with pastry blender or fork until crumbly. Lightly beat egg yolk and combine with sour cream in separate bowl; add to flour mixture. Stir vigorously until dough leaves side of bowl.

Place on lightly floured board; knead 1 minute. Divide dough into thirds, forming each into a flat circle; cover with plastic wrap. Chill for 8 hours or up to several days.

Preheat oven to 350°. Roll each third out to form a 12-inch circle; cut into 12 equal wedges. Place 1 teaspoon preserves on wide end of each wedge. Starting at wide end, roll to tip. Brush tip with beaten egg white; form into crescent shape. Place on baking sheet, pointed-seam-side down.

Bake 20 to 25 minutes or until golden. Remove and cool on wire rack. Sprinkle with confectioners' sugar.

Makes approximately 3 dozen

Ham Rolls

2½ cups flour
1 tablespoon baking
   powder
1 teaspoon salt
½ cup sour cream
4 to 6 tablespoons milk
4 tablespoons vegetable oil
1 egg yolk
2 small egg whites, divided,
   slightly beaten
2 cups diced cooked ham
2 sweet gherkins, minced

Preheat oven to 375°. Grease a 10 x 15-inch cookie sheet.

Sift flour and baking powder into a large bowl. Stir in salt, sour cream, milk, oil, egg yolk, and 1 egg white. Combine ingredients using a wooden spoon or the dough hook of an electric mixer. If using mixer, combine ingredients on highest speed for 1 minute.

Turn out dough onto a lightly floured board. Roll out dough to a ½-inch thickness; cut out 2 x 4-inch rectangles. Brush with remaining egg white.

Combine ham and pickles in a small bowl. Place a tablespoonful of the mixture on each rectangle of dough; roll rectangles up, jelly-roll style, beginning on a short side. Place on cookie sheet.

Brush rolls with milk. Bake for 15 minutes or until golden brown. Cool slightly before serving.

Makes 1 dozen

Apple Pastries

2 pounds apples, peeled and chopped into small pieces
½ cup raisins
¼ cup sugar
1 tablespoon lemon juice
2¾ cups flour
1 teaspoon baking powder
⅓ cup sugar
¼ teaspoon salt
¾ cup sour cream
6 tablespoons milk
6 tablespoons vegetable oil
1 teaspoon vanilla
Milk
Icing

Combine apples, raisins, ¼ cup sugar, and lemon juice in a small saucepan. Simmer over medium heat, stirring often until apples are soft. Set aside to cool.

Preheat oven to 375°. Sift flour and baking powder into a large bowl. Stir in ⅓ cup sugar, salt, sour cream, milk, oil, and vanilla. Combine the ingredients using a wooden spoon or the dough hook of an electric mixer. If using mixer, combine ingredients on the highest setting for 1 minute.

Roll out dough on a lightly floured board to about a ¼-inch thickness. Cut out 3-inch circles with cookie cutter or sharp knife. Place a tablespoonful of the apple mixture in the center of half the circles. Brush the edges of the filled circles with milk.

Cover the filled circles with the remaining circle; press the edges firmly together. Place pastries on a 10 x 15-inch non-stick cookie sheet. Bake for 15 minutes or until golden brown.

Prepare Icing while pastries are baking. Remove pastries from pan and cool on wire rack. Drizzle icing over pastries.

Note: Cherries, peaches, or apricots can be substituted for apples. If desired, spread ½ to 1 cup of chopped almonds over fruit mixture.

Makes 10 to 12 servings

Poppy Lattice Tart

½ cup milk
1 cup sugar, divided
4 tablespoons butter *or* margarine
3 cups ground poppy seed
1 teaspoon ground cinnamon
1 egg
4 tablespoons whipping cream
5 tablespoons brandy
1 cup raisins
2¾ cups flour
1 teaspoon baking powder
¼ teaspoon salt
¾ cup sour cream
5 tablespoons milk
5 tablespoons vegetable oil
1 teaspoon vanilla
Milk
Glaze

Place ½ cup milk, ¾ cup sugar, and butter in a saucepan; bring to a boil, stirring occasionally. Remove from heat; stir in poppy seed, cinnamon, egg, cream, brandy, and raisins. Set aside to cool.

Sift flour and baking powder into a large bowl. Stir in remaining sugar, salt, sour cream, milk, oil, and vanilla. Combine ingredients using a wooden spoon or the dough hook of an electric mixer. If using mixer, combine ingredients on highest speed for 1 minute.

Preheat oven to 375°. Grease the bottom of an 8-inch springform pan.

Turn out dough onto a lightly floured board. Shape into a roll. Divide roll into 5 equal pieces. Roll out 1 piece into an 8-inch circle. Place circle in bottom of springform pan. Roll out a second piece of dough to form a long rectangle large enough to fit around the inside of the pan. Line the sides with the rolled out rectangle; press gently to attach it to the base.

Spread the dough base with ⅓ the poppy seed mixture. Roll out another piece of dough into an 8-inch circle; place over poppy seed mixture. Spread ⅓ poppy seed mixture over this layer of dough. Repeat process with 1 piece of dough and remaining poppy seed mixture.

Roll out remaining piece of dough into an 8-inch square. Cut into ½-inch strips. Place strips over top of tart to form a lattice pattern. Brush top of tart with milk.

Bake for 50 minutes or until golden brown. Prepare Glaze while tart is baking. Brush Glaze over tart as soon as it is removed from oven. Remove from pan and cool on wire rack.

Makes 8 to 10 servings

Butter Almond Cake

2½ cups flour
1 teaspoon baking powder
⅔ cup sugar, divided
¾ cup sour cream
6 tablespoons milk
6 tablespoons vegetable oil
2 teaspoons vanilla, divided
¾ cup raisins
½ cup butter *or* margarine, cut into small pieces
½ cup slivered almonds

Preheat oven to 375°. Grease a 9 x 13-inch baking pan.

Sift flour and baking powder into a large bowl. Stir in ⅓ cup sugar, sour cream, milk, oil, and 1 teaspoon vanilla. Combine ingredients using a wooden spoon or the dough hook of an electric mixer. If using mixer, combine ingredients on highest setting for 1 minute.

Turn out dough onto a lightly floured board; shape into a roll. Knead in raisins. Spread dough in prepared pan.

Sprinkle butter pieces over dough. Combine remaining sugar, vanilla, and almonds in small bowl. Sprinkle evenly over dough.

Bake for 20 to 25 minutes or until golden brown. Remove from pan and cool on wire rack. Cut into squares before serving.

Makes 10 to 12 servings

Miniature Pecan Rolls

3 cups flour
½ cup sugar
1 teaspoon salt
1 package active dry yeast
½ cup cream *or* milk
¾ cup butter
½ cup sour cream
2 eggs, slightly beaten
¼ cup butter *or* margarine, melted and divided
½ cup sugar mixed with 1 teaspoon cinnamon
½ cup chopped nuts
½ cup currants
1½ cups pecan halves

Combine flour, ½ cup sugar, salt, and yeast in bowl. Heat cream in saucepan; stir in ¾ cup butter until melted. Combine sour cream and eggs in small bowl. Stir cream mixture and sour cream mixture into flour until well blended. Cover and chill overnight.

Preheat oven to 350°. Divide dough into 4 parts. Roll each part out to form a 3 x 12-inch rectangle. Brush each rectangle with 1 tablespoon melted butter; sprinkle with 2 tablespoons sugar-cinnamon mixture. Spread with 2 tablespoons chopped nuts and 2 tablespoons currants.

Roll each piece tightly beginning on a long side; cut into 12 slices. Repeat with remaining dough and filling. Place 2 pecan halves in bottom of each of 48 miniature cupcake liners.

Syrup

Prepare Syrup; pour ½ teaspoon over pecans. Top with slice of dough.

Bake 15 to 20 minutes or until golden. Cool slightly and remove from liners.

Makes approximately 4 dozen

Syrup

2 tablespoons light corn syrup
1 cup firmly packed light brown sugar
¼ cup butter
1 tablespoon water

Bring all ingredients to boil in saucepan; stir to blend.

Stollen

(Illustrated on pp. 234-235)

3½ to 4 cups flour
1 teaspoon baking powder
¾ cup sugar
1 teaspoon vanilla
¼ teaspoon salt
¼ teaspoon each ground cloves, cardamom, ginger, nutmeg, and cinnamon
Zest of ½ lemon
2 eggs
½ cup butter *or* margarine at room temperature
1 cup sour cream
1 cup peeled, ground almonds
½ cup diced candied lemon peel
½ cup diced candied orange peel
1½ cups raisins, soaked overnight in ⅓ cup dark rum
⅓ cup melted butter *or* margarine
1 cup confectioners' sugar

Preheat oven to 400°.

Sift flour and baking powder into a large bowl. Stir in sugar, vanilla, salt, spices, and zest. Add eggs, 1 at a time, beating well after each addition. Blend in butter and sour cream. Combine the ingredients with a wooden spoon or the dough hook of an electric mixer. If using mixer, begin on the lowest setting to blend, then adjust to high. Mix until well blended.

Turn out dough on a lightly floured board and knead in the almonds and candied lemon and orange peel. Knead in raisins. Form the dough into a somewhat flat loaf shape and place it on a 10 x 15-inch non-stick cookie sheet.

Bake for 50 to 60 minutes, or until golden brown and crusty.

Brush the cake immediately after baking with melted butter and dust with sugar. Remove from pan and cool completely on wire rack.

Makes 10 to 12 servings

Fruit and Nut Slices

2¾ cups flour
1 teaspoon baking powder
½ cup sour cream
6 tablespoons milk
6 tablespoons vegetable oil
1 teaspoon vanilla
¼ teaspoon salt
⅓ cup butter *or* margarine at room temperature
2 cups almond paste (available at gourmet stores)
2½ cups raisins
1 cup chopped hazelnuts
½ cup diced candied lemon peel
¼ teaspoon ground cinnamon
2 tablespoons dark rum
Milk
Apricot Glaze
Icing
Sliced, toasted almonds

Preheat oven to 375°. Grease a 10 x 15-inch jelly-roll pan.

Sift flour and baking powder into a large bowl. Stir in sour cream, milk, oil, vanilla, and salt. Combine ingredients using a wooden spoon or the dough hook of an electric mixer. If using mixer, combine ingredients on highest setting for 1 minute.

Turn out dough onto a lightly floured board. Roll out to form a 10 x 20-inch rectangle. Spread ½ the butter over dough. Set dough aside.

Knead almond paste until soft. Roll out paste to form two 10-inch squares. Place them side by side atop the dough. Spread the almond paste with remaining butter.

Combine raisins, hazelnuts, lemon peel, cinnamon, and rum in a bowl. Spread the mixture over the dough; press down lightly with hand. Cut the dough in half to form two 10-inch squares. Roll up each square jelly-roll style. Place the rolls side by side on prepared pan.

Cut a 7-inch long by ½-inch deep slash down the middle of each roll. Brush the rolls with milk. Bake for 20 to 30 minutes or until lightly browned. Prepare Apricot Glaze and Icing while rolls are baking.

Remove rolls from oven and brush first with Apricot Glaze and then with Icing. Sprinkle with almonds. Cool rolls on wire rack; slice before serving.

Makes approximately 20 slices

Apricot Glaze

¼ cup apricot jam
2 tablespoons water

Combine jam and water in small saucepan. Bring mixture to a boil, stirring until blended. Remove from heat.

Icing

1 cup confectioners' sugar
2 to 4 tablespoons orange juice

Combine sugar and enough orange juice in a small bowl to make a smooth consistency.

Puff Pastry
and
French Pastries

Puff Pastry

Before using frozen puff pastry, always remove it from the freezer and thaw completely at room temperature.

When rolling out puff pastry, place it on a lightly floured surface and roll it back and forth in two directions, top to bottom, and left to right. The dough will not rise evenly when baked if rolled in only one direction.

Use a sharp knife or pastry cutter to cut dough evenly.

Any leftover dough can be stacked together and rerolled. Cut out small shapes for decoration.

Sprinkle the baking sheet with cold water before placing pastry on it. The water creates steam during baking to help the pastry rise.

Easy Napoleons

1 10-ounce package frozen patty shells, thawed in refrigerator overnight
1 3¾-ounce package instant French vanilla pudding mix
1 cup confectioners' sugar
½ teaspoon hot water
½ teaspoon vanilla
1 ounce unsweetened chocolate, melted

Preheat oven to 400°.

Remove 2 patty shells from refrigerator at a time; press together on lightly floured board. Roll into 5 x 9-inch rectangle. Cut into four 2¼ x 5-inch slices. Repeat with rest of patty shells.

Place slices 1 inch apart on a 10 x 15-inch cookie sheet; chill for 30 minutes. Prick with tines of fork every ¼ inch. Bake for 12 to 15 minutes until golden. Cool on wire rack.

Prepare pudding mix using ½ cup less milk than directions specify; set aside. Stir together confectioners' sugar, water, and vanilla in bowl to make a thin glaze.

Spread glaze on top of 8 rectangles. Before glaze dries, dip toothpick into chocolate and make thin lines ½ inch apart the length of rectangle. Draw toothpick across lines, alternating from side to side to give rippled effect.

Spread pudding on the remaining 16 rectangles; assemble Napoleons in 3 layers with glazed rectangle on top.

Makes 8 servings

Dutch Cherry Gateau

(Illustrated on pp. 202-203)

1 17¼-ounce package frozen puff pastry, thawed to room temperature
1 17-ounce can dark, sweet, pitted cherries
1 tablespoon cornstarch
2 teaspoons sugar
½ cup cherry jelly
1 tablespoon water
½ cup sifted confectioners' sugar, divided
2 cups whipping cream

Arrange puff pastry in one flat layer and roll out on lightly floured board. Cut out three 10-inch circles. Place pastry circles on 10 x 15-inch cookie sheets that have been sprinkled lightly with water; prick with a fork. Set aside for 15 minutes. Preheat oven to 425°.

Bake pastry circles for 10 to 15 minutes or until puffy and golden. Remove the circles from the cooking sheets; cool on wire rack. Cut off ¼-inch around the edges with a pointed knife to expose flaky layers.

Drain cherries and reserve ½ cup of the cherry juice. Place cornstarch in small saucepan and whisk in cherry juice. Bring juice to a boil. Continue cooking for 2 minutes, whisking often until mixture thickens slightly. Stir in cherries and sugar, reserving 6 cherries for decoration. Set aside to cool, stirring occasionally. Taste and add sugar if desired.

Heat jelly in a small saucepan with 1 tablespoon water. Stir until jelly is melted; cool for 5 minutes.

Brush jelly lightly over tops of 2 of the pastry circles. Blend ¼ cup confectioners' sugar with remaining jelly and spread over remaining circle. Reserve this circle to use last.

Beat whipping cream until soft peaks form, sprinkle with remaining confectioners' sugar. Continue beating until stiff peaks form. Spoon whipped cream into pastry bag fitted with a star tip. Place one circle on serving platter. Pipe a thick ring of cream around outer edges. Spoon ½ the cherries into the center. Place second circle gently over first; pipe with whipped cream. Fill the center with cherries. Place the reserved circle on top. Garnish with 6 rosettes of whipped cream; place a cherry on each rosette.

For best results, assemble gateau just before serving. Use a serrated knife to cut into wedges.

Makes 6 to 8 servings

Apricot Pastries

1 17¼-ounce package
  frozen puff pastry,
  thawed to room
  temperature
3 cups canned apricot
  halves, drained
  Almond slivers
1 egg yolk beaten with 1
  tablespoon milk
  Apricot Glaze

Preheat oven to 425°.

Arrange puff pastry in a flat layer. Roll out pastry to form a 20 x 12-inch rectangle and cut out 3-inch squares or 3-inch circles. Drain apricots and arrange 1 in the center of each pastry piece. Place pastry on a cookie sheet that has been sprinkled lightly with water. Sprinkle with almonds.

For *pinwheels*, make a 1¼-inch cut from each corner toward the center. Fold every other point toward the center. Press ends together to seal in center.

For *oblongs*, fold two corners toward the center and pinch together.

For *puffs*, fold all edges toward the center and press down.

Brush pastries lightly with egg yolk mixture.

Bake for 10 to 15 minutes or until golden brown. Prepare Apricot Glaze while pastries are baking. Remove pastries from oven; place on wire rack. Brush glaze over pastries; set aside to cool.

Makes approximately 2 dozen pastries

Apricot Glaze

½ cup apricot jam
3 tablespoons water

Combine jam and water in a small saucepan and bring to a boil, stirring to blend. Set aside.

Apricot Pastries, this page

Raspberries and Cream

1 17¼-ounce package
   frozen puff pastry shells,
   thawed to room
   temperature
2 cups fresh raspberries,
   washed and drained on
   paper towels
1 cup whipping cream
¼ cup confectioners' sugar,
   sifted

Preheat oven to 375°.

Place thawed shells on 10 x 15-inch non-stick cookie sheet that has been lightly sprinkled with water. Brush tops with water. Bake for 5 minutes; remove tops and place beside shells on cookie sheet. Bake 10 to 15 minutes longer or until shells are golden brown and puffed.

Place on wire rack to cool. Remove any uncooked dough from center of shells.

Place 2 tablespoons of raspberries in each shell. Reserve some of the berries for decoration. Purée ½ cup berries. Whip cream until soft peaks form. Sprinkle with sugar and continue beating until stiff peaks form. Fold in puréed berries. Mound whipped cream mixture into pastry shells. Garnish with reserved raspberries. Arrange tops on side of serving dish.

Note: For best results, assemble pastries close to serving time. Strawberries, currants, blackberries, or stewed cranberries can be used instead of raspberries.

Makes 8 servings

Sweet Ovals

1 sheet frozen puff pastry,
   thawed
   Sugar

Roll out pastry on a surface sprinkled with sugar to ⅛-inch thickness. Use a 2-inch round cookie cutter to cut out circles. Gather scraps together and reroll. Cut out additional cookies.

Sprinkle work surface with sugar and turn circles upside down. Stretch each circle into an oval. Prick well with a fork.

Place pastries on a 10 x 15-inch cookie sheet. Refrigerate for 15 minutes. Preheat oven to 400°.

Bake for 7 to 8 minutes or until golden, watching carefully to avoid burning. Remove from cookie sheet to wire racks; cool completely. Store in airtight container.

Makes approximately 3 dozen cookies

Raspberries and Cream, this page

Elephant Ears

17¼-ounce package
   frozen puff pastry,
   thawed to room
   temperature
2 tablespoons butter *or*
   margarine, melted and
   cooled
   Sugar

Sprinkle puff pastry with sugar. Roll out pastry on a sugar-sprinkled board to form a 20 x 8-inch rectangle. Brush with cooled butter. Sprinkle sugar over the pastry.

Brush edges of pastry with water. Roll each short end toward the center until both rolls touch. Gently press rolls together. Chill for 1 hour.

Preheat oven to 400°. Cut chilled rolls into ¼-inch slices. Sprinkle cut sides with sugar. Place slices 1½ inches apart on a 10 x 15-inch non-stick cookie sheet that has been lightly sprinkled with water. Flatten each slice lightly with a spatula.

Bake for 15 to 20 minutes or until puffy and golden brown. Turn pastries over with spatula; cool on cookie sheet.

Makes 12 pastries

Cream Filled Cookies

1 17¼-ounce package
   frozen puff pastry,
   thawed to room
   temperature
   Sugar
1 cup whipping cream,
   chilled
¼ cup confectioners' sugar
1 teaspoon vanilla

Preheat oven to 400°.

Roll out pastry to a ¼-inch thickness. Cut out 2-inch circles; sprinkle both sides with sugar. Place on 10 x 15-inch non-stick cookie sheet that has been lightly sprinkled with water.

Bake for 10 minutes or until golden brown. Remove from cookie sheet; cool on wire rack.

Whip cream in bowl until soft peaks form. Sprinkle with confectioners' sugar and vanilla. Continue beating until stiff peaks form.

Spoon whipped cream into pastry bag and pipe cream onto the flat side of half the cookies. Top with remaining cookies.

Note: For best results, assemble close to serving time.

Makes 8 servings

French Pastries

French pastries such as cream puffs and eclairs are made with a paste-type dough called *pate a choux*. The *choux* paste is made of flour, cornstarch, water, butter, eggs, and baking powder. When baked, the dough expands in size as air forms in the center of the puff or eclair.

The Individual Steps

1 Lightly grease the pan with butter, margarine, or vegetable oil.

2 Sprinkle with flour.

3 Move the pan back and forth to evenly distribute the flour.

4 Sift the flour and cornstarch together.

5 An easy method is to sift the flour and cornstarch onto a piece of waxed paper that can easily be lifted and used to pour the mixture.

1 Place the water and butter in a saucepan.

2 Bring to a boil.

3 Remove from heat and immediately add the flour mixture all at once.

4 Stir with a wooden spoon.

5 Do not add the flour a little at a time, or the mixture will tend to lump.

1 Vigorously beat the flour into the boiling water.

2 Return the pan to the heat.

3 Continue to stir mixture for 1 to 2 minutes.

1 Beat the mixture until it becomes smooth.

2 It will begin to pull away from the sides of the pan and will form a smooth ball.

3 When the ball is smoothly formed, it will not cling to the pan.

1 Take the pan off the heat.

2 Turn the dough into a bowl.

3 Set the bowl aside at room temperature to cool for 3 minutes.

4 Do not cool the dough any longer than 3 minutes, or it will lose too much of the warmth needed to blend with the remaining ingredients.

1 Have the eggs at room temperature.

2 Break each egg into a cup to check for freshness before adding to the hot dough.

3 Beat well after adding each egg, until the egg is fully blended into the mixture.

1 Continue to beat in the eggs until the dough is shiny and smooth.

2 The proper consistency for the dough is reached when a small amount of dough will hang on the end of a spoon.

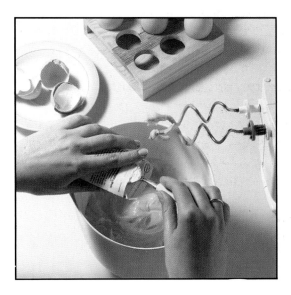

1 Add the baking powder last.

2 Blend in the baking powder completely.

1 Shape the dough or pipe it as directed in the recipe.

2 The dough is now ready to be baked.

Baking

Bake the French pastries according to the recipe directions. Bake for the proper amount of time listed in the recipe or until the pastries are golden and puffy, yet firm to the touch. *Do not* open the oven door before the minimum amount of baking time given in the recipe has passed. This will help to prevent the pastries from collapsing. When the pastries are done, remove them from the pan and cool on a wire rack in a draft-free area before filling. Use a sharp knife to cut open the pastries and remove any uncooked dough.

Cream Puffs

(Illustrated on pp. 212-213)

1 cup flour
2 tablespoons cornstarch
1 cup water
6 tablespoons butter *or* margarine
4 eggs at room temperature
1 teaspoon baking powder
Fruit Filling
Cream Filling
Confectioners' sugar
Flaked almonds

Preheat oven to 400°. Grease and flour a 10x15-inch cookie sheet.

Sift flour and cornstarch together; set aside. Bring water and butter to a boil in saucepan. Remove from heat; add flour and cornstarch all at once. Return to heat; beat with a wooden spoon for 1 to 2 minutes until mixture pulls away from the sides of pan and forms a ball. Remove from heat and turn dough into a bowl; cool for 3 minutes. Add eggs, one at a time, beating well after each addition. Beat until shiny and smooth and a small amount of dough will hang from the end of a spoon. Stir baking powder into the dough.

Drop dough by large spoonfuls or use pastry bag without a tip to pipe puffs about 3 inches apart onto prepared cookie sheet. Bake for 35 to 40 minutes or until golden and puffy, yet firm to the touch. Remove from pan; cool on wire rack in a draft-free area. Prepare Fruit and Cream Fillings.

Slice tops off puffs. Remove any uncooked dough. Spoon Fruit Filling into cream puffs. Pipe Cream Filling into puffs. Replace lids; dust with sugar and sprinkle with almonds.

For best results, assemble just before serving.

Makes 12 cream puffs

Fruit Filling

2 cups sour cherries *or* strawberries, washed and drained
¼ cup sugar
2 tablespoons water
1 tablespoon cornstarch

Combine cherries, sugar, and water in a saucepan. Bring just to a boil. Remove cherries; set aside. Measure juice in pan; add water as needed to measure ½ cup. Blend juice with cornstarch and return to a boil, stirring until mixture begins to thicken. Stir in cherries. Set aside to cool.

Cream Filling

2 cups whipping cream, chilled
¼ cup confectioners' sugar
1 teaspoon vanilla

Beat cream until soft peaks form. Sprinkle with sugar and vanilla. Continue beating until stiff peaks form.

Flaky Gateau

Kneaded Dough Base
Flaky Pastry
Cherry Filling
Cream Filling
¼ cup red currant jelly
1 teaspoon water
Confectioners' sugar

Prepare the Kneaded Dough Base, Flaky Pastry, Cherry Filling and Cream Filling.

To Assemble: Heat jelly and water in a small saucepan, stirring until melted. Brush the Kneaded Dough Base thinly with red currant jelly. Top with 1 layer of Flaky Pastry. Spread Flaky Pastry layer with ½ the Cherry Filling and ⅓ the Cream Filling.

Place the second Flaky Pastry layer on top. Spread with the remaining Cherry Filling and Cream Filling. Crumble the third Flaky Pastry layer and sprinkle it over the Cream Filling. Dust with confectioners' sugar. Serve immediately.

Makes 8 servings

Kneaded Dough Base

1¼ cups flour
¼ cup sugar
4 tablespoons butter *or* margarine
3 tablespoons vegetable shortening
1 teaspoon vanilla
3 to 5 tablespoons ice water

Combine all ingredients except water in a large bowl using a wooden spoon or the dough hook of an electric mixer. If using dough hook, begin on the lowest speed to blend then adjust to high. Add just enough ice water while beating to form dough into a ball. Turn dough out onto lightly floured board and knead until smooth. Cover with plastic wrap; chill for 30 minutes.

Preheat oven to 300°. Grease and flour the bottom of an 8-inch round cake pan.

Pat dough into the prepared pan. Prick several times with a fork. Bake for 15 minutes or until crust is golden. Remove from pan; cool crust on cake plate.

(continued on next page)

Flaky Pastry

1 cup flour
2 tablespoons cornstarch
1 cup water
6 tablespoons butter *or* margarine
4 eggs at room temperature
1 teaspoon baking powder

Preheat oven to 400°. Grease three 8-inch round cake pans.

Sift flour and cornstarch together; set aside. Bring water and butter to a boil in saucepan. Remove from heat; add flour and cornstarch all at once. Return to heat; beat with a wooden spoon for 1 to 2 minutes or until mixture leaves the sides of the pan and forms a ball. Remove from heat and turn dough into a bowl; add eggs, one at a time, beating well after each addition. Beat until shiny and smooth and a small amount of dough will hang from the end of a spoon. Stir baking powder into the cooled dough.

Spread ⅓ of the dough into each cake pan. Take care that the dough is not too thin at the edges or it will burn.

Bake for 20 to 25 minutes or until lightly browned. Loosen the layer from the pan immediately after baking; set aside to cool on a wire rack so steam will evaporate.

Cherry Filling

1 cup pitted, canned sweet cherries, drained and juice reserved
2 tablespoons cornstarch
2 teaspoons sugar

Measure reserved juice; add water as needed to measure 1 cup. Combine 4 tablespoons of juice with cornstarch in small bowl. Bring remaining juice to a boil in a saucepan; remove from heat and stir in cornstarch mixture. Bring juice to a boil. Stir in cherries and sugar; set aside to cool.

Cream Filling

2 cups whipping cream, chilled
¼ cup confectioners' sugar
1 teaspoon vanilla

Whip cream in a large bowl until soft peaks form. Sprinkle with sugar and vanilla. Continue beating until stiff peaks form.

Flaky Gateau, this page

Eclairs

1 cup flour
2 tablespoons cornstarch
1 cup water
6 tablespoons butter *or* margarine
4 eggs at room temperature
1 teaspoon baking powder
  Whipped Cream Filling
¼ cup apricot jam

Preheat oven to 400°. Grease and flour a 10 x 15-inch cookie sheet.

Sift flour and cornstarch together; set aside. Bring water and butter to a boil in saucepan. Remove from heat; add flour and cornstarch all at once. Return to heat; beat with a wooden spoon for 1 to 2 minutes or until mixture leaves the sides of the pan and forms a ball. Remove from heat. Turn dough into a bowl. Cool for 3 minutes. Add eggs, 1 at a time, beating well after each addition. Beat until shiny and smooth and a small amount of dough will hang from the end of a spoon. Stir baking powder into the dough.

Spoon dough into a pastry bag with a star tip; pipe out 1-inch wide by 2½-inch long strips onto prepared cookie sheet. Bake for 20 minutes or until golden and puffy.

Cut top off each eclair immediately after baking; remove any uncooked dough. Place on wire rack to cool. Prepare Whipped Cream Filling. Heat jam in small pan, until warm.

Spoon whipped cream into pastry bag with a star tip and pipe into the eclairs. Replace top on each one. Brush tops with jam. Serve immediately.

Makes 8 servings

Whipped Cream Filling

1 cup whipping cream, chilled
4 tablespoons light brown sugar

Whip cream until soft peaks form. Sprinkle with sugar. Continue beating until stiff peaks form.

Cranberry Ring

1 cup flour
2 tablespoons cornstarch
1 cup water
6 tablespoons butter *or* margarine
4 eggs at room temperature
1 teaspoon baking powder
    Cranberry Filling
    Confectioners' sugar

Preheat oven to 400°. Grease and flour a 10 x 15-inch cookie sheet.

Sift flour and cornstarch together; set aside. Bring water and butter to a boil in saucepan. Remove from heat; add flour and cornstarch all at once. Return to heat; beat with a wooden spoon for 1 to 2 minutes or until mixture leaves the sides of the pan and forms a ball. Remove from heat; turn dough into a bowl. Add eggs, 1 at a time, beating well after each addition. Beat until shiny and smooth and a small amount of dough will hang from the end of a spoon. Stir baking powder into the dough.

Spoon dough into a pastry bag fitted with a star tip. Pipe out half the dough into an 8-inch wide ring. Pipe out remaining dough into 2 more circles inside the ring. Make each circle touch the previous one. Bake for 20 to 25 minutes or until golden and puffy. *Do not* open the oven door during the first 15 minutes of baking or the ring will collapse.

Slice the top off the ring as soon as it is removed from oven. Cool on wire rack. Remove any uncooked dough inside the ring. Prepare Cranberry Filling while ring is cooling. Spoon the Cranberry Filling over the bottom half of the ring. Place the lid on top; dust with sugar. Serve immediately.

Makes 8 servings

Cranberry Filling

2 cups whipping cream, chilled
2 tablespoons sugar
1 teaspoon vanilla
2 ounces semi-sweet chocolate, grated
1 cup canned cranberries, drained

Whip cream until soft peaks form. Sprinkle with sugar and vanilla. Continue beating until stiff peaks form. Gently fold in the chocolate and cranberries.

Cheesy Cream Puffs

1 cup flour
2 tablespoons cornstarch
1 cup water
6 tablespoons butter *or* margarine
4 eggs at room temperature
1 teaspoon baking powder
½ cup butter *or* margarine at room temperature
4 ounces Roquefort cheese at room temperature
1 cup whipping cream, chilled
   Chopped parsley
   Caraway seed
   Poppy seed

Preheat oven to 400°. Grease and flour a 10 x 15-inch cookie sheet.

Sift flour and cornstarch together; set aside. Bring water and 6 tablespoons butter to a boil in saucepan. Remove from heat; add flour and cornstarch all at once. Return to heat; beat with a wooden spoon for 1 to 2 minutes or until mixture leaves the sides of the pan and forms a ball. Remove from heat; turn dough into a bowl. Add eggs, 1 at a time, beating well after each addition. Beat until shiny and smooth and a small amount of dough will hang from the end of a spoon. Stir baking powder into the dough.

Spoon dough into a pastry bag fitted with a narrow star tip and pipe 1-inch mounds onto the prepared cookie sheet. Bake for 20 minutes or until golden and puffy. *Do not* open the oven door during the first 15 minutes of baking time or the pastries will collapse.

Slice off a small lid from each cream puff as soon as they are removed from oven. Remove from pan and cool on wire rack. Remove any uncooked dough inside the ring.

Cream remaining butter and Roquefort cheese in a small bowl; set aside. Whip cream until stiff peaks form. Fold ¾ of the whipped cream into cheese mixture. Fill puffs with cheese mixture. Spread the lids thinly with remaining whipped cream and sprinkle with parsley, caraway seed, and poppy seed. Place the lids on the puffs.

Makes 8 to 10 servings

Deep Frying French Pastries and Other Dough

Several types of dough work well when deep fried. They include French pastries, kneaded dough, sour cream dough, and yeast dough.

If you have a deep skillet with high sides, this can be used for deep frying, or a deep dutch oven or kettle will also work. If you use an electric deep fryer, be sure to follow the manufacturer's instructions for the proper use and handling.

One of the most important things to know about deep frying is the proper kind of oil to use. Neutral-flavored 100% vegetable oils and shortenings are excellent for deep frying. Both the oils and shortenings have high smoking points and foods will not burn as easily. Bring the oil to the proper temperature slowly so that any moisture can evaporate.

The ideal deep-frying temperature is 365° to 375°. Use the frying temperature called for in the recipe. The oil should not be too hot or too cold. If it is too hot, the pastries will not rise properly and will brown too quickly. They may also be sticky and partially uncooked in the middle. If the oil is too cold, the pastry absorbs too much oil and may begin to break apart. As you add more pastries to the oil, the temperature will begin to cool, so fry in small batches in order to maintain an even temperature.

Always slide the pastries gently into the oil to avoid splashing and burning. Skim out any crumbs or bits of burned food between frying each batch and give the oil time to return to the proper temperature before frying each new batch.

Remove cooked pastries from the hot oil with a slotted spoon or strainer. Drain on paper towels. Serve warm or set aside to cool.

Cookie Knots

---

3 cups flour
1 teaspoon baking powder
½ cup sugar
2 tablespoons dark rum
3 eggs
½ cup butter *or* margarine at
   room temperature

Sift flour and baking powder into a large bowl. Add sugar, rum, eggs, and butter. Combine ingredients using a wooden spoon or the dough hook of an electric mixer. If using a mixer, begin on low to blend, then adjust mixer to high for 5 minutes. Blend in enough milk or water to make a dough that will hold together. Turn out dough onto a lightly floured

4 to 6 tablespoons milk *or*
water
Vegetable oil
Confectioners' sugar,
sifted

board; knead until smooth. Form dough into a ball; cover with plastic wrap or foil. Chill for 30 minutes.

Roll out dough to a ¼-inch thickness on a lightly floured board; cut into strips. Cut a slash in the middle of each strip; pull one end through the cut.

Heat oil in a deep skillet with high sides or use a deep-fat fryer heated to 375°.

Gently slide cookies into the hot oil, a few at a time. Fry until golden brown. Remove with a slotted spoon; drain on paper towels. Dust with sugar.

Makes approximately 2 dozen

Deep-Fried Cookies

2 cups flour
1 teaspoon baking powder
1 tablespoon sugar
1 teaspoon vanilla
¼ teaspoon salt
1 egg
2 tablespoons brandy
2 tablespoons water
Milk
Vegetable oil
Confectioners' sugar,
sifted

Sift flour and baking powder into a large bowl. Add sugar, vanilla, salt, egg, brandy, and water. Combine ingredients using a wooden spoon or the dough hook of an electric mixer. If using mixer, begin on low to blend, then adjust mixer to high for 5 minutes. Place dough on a lightly floured board; knead until smooth.

Roll out dough to a ¼-inch thickness; cut out 2½-inch circles. On each circle, cut 4 slashes from edge toward center, 1 slash every quarter of the way around. *Do not* cut through center. Brush the centers of half the cookies with milk. Place remaining cookies on top, arranging them so that the top slashes are between the slashes on the bottom. Press gently together in center.

Heat oil in a deep skillet with high sides or use a deep-fat fryer heated to 375°.

Slide cookies gently into hot oil, a few at a time. Press them in the center with the tip of a spoon to make a hollow. Deep fry until golden brown on both sides. Remove with a slotted spoon. Drain on paper towels. Dust with confectioners' sugar.

Makes approximately 1 dozen

Sour Cream Pastries

½ cup sour cream
1 tablespoon cornstarch
¼ cup sugar
1 egg
½ teaspoon almond extract
½ cup ground almonds
¼ cup raisins
2 cups flour
1 teaspoon baking powder
½ cup sour cream
5 tablespoons milk
1 egg yolk
½ egg white
5 tablespoons vegetable oil
¼ teaspoon salt
   Egg white
   Vegetable oil
¼ cup sugar
1 teaspoon ground
   cinnamon

Combine first 7 ingredients in a bowl and set aside.

Sift flour and baking powder into a large bowl. Add remaining sour cream, milk, egg yolk, egg white, 5 tablespoons oil, and salt. Combine the ingredients using a wooden spoon or the dough hook of an electric mixer set on high for about 1 minute. Shape into a ball; place on a lightly floured board.

Roll out dough to a ½-inch thickness; cut into 3-inch circles. Place a small amount of the sour cream mixture onto half of the circles. Brush the edges with egg white. Place the remaining circles on top of them; press the edges together.

Heat oil in a deep skillet with high sides or use a deep-fat fryer heated to 375°.

Deep fry the pastries in the hot oil, a few at a time, until they are light brown on both sides. Remove them with a slotted spoon; drain well on paper towels. Combine sugar with cinnamon. While still warm, sprinkle pastries with sugar-cinnamon mixture.

Makes 8 servings

Crullers

(Illustrated on pp. 226-227)

1 cup flour
2 tablespoons cornstarch
1 cup water
¼ cup butter *or* margarine
4 tablespoons sugar
1 teaspoon vanilla
4 eggs at room temperature
1 teaspoon baking powder
   Vegetable oil
   Lemon Icing

Sift flour and cornstarch together; set aside. Bring water and butter to a boil in saucepan. Remove from heat; add flour and cornstarch all at once. Return to heat; beat with a wooden spoon for 1 to 2 minutes or until mixture leaves the sides of the pan and forms a ball. Remove from heat and turn dough into a bowl. Blend in sugar and vanilla. Add eggs, 1 at a time, beating well after each addition. Beat until shiny and smooth and a small amount of dough will hang from the end of a spoon. Stir baking powder into the dough.

Spoon dough into a pastry bag fitted with a wide tip and pipe out dough into 1½ x 3-inch strips onto greased parchment paper.

Heat oil in a deep skillet with high sides or deep-fat fryer heated to 375°.

Fry by sliding dough gently into the oil a few at a time. Fry until they are light brown on both sides. Remove with a slotted spoon; drain on paper towels.

Prepare Lemon Icing and spread over crullers.

Variation: Pipe dough into rings to form traditional doughnut shapes.

Makes 18 servings

Lemon Icing

2 cups confectioners' sugar, sifted
3 tablespoons lemon juice
2 to 4 tablespoons hot water

Mix sugar with lemon juice in a small bowl. Stir in enough hot water to make icing spreadable.

Raisin Fritters

1 cup flour
2 tablespoons cornstarch
1 cup water
¼ cup butter *or* margarine
4 eggs at room temperature
1 teaspoon baking powder
½ cup raisins
  Vegetable oil
  Confectioners' sugar

Sift flour and cornstarch together; set aside. Bring water and butter to a boil in saucepan. Remove from heat; add flour and cornstarch all at once. Return to heat; beat with a wooden spoon for 1 to 2 minutes until mixture leaves the sides of the pan and forms a ball. Remove from heat; turn dough into a bowl. Add eggs, 1 at a time, beating well after each addition. Beat until shiny and smooth and a small amount of dough will hang from the end of a spoon. Stir baking powder into the dough. Mix in raisins.

Heat oil in a deep skillet with high sides or use a deep-fat fryer heated to 375°.

Use a teaspoon to form balls of dough. Gently slide fritters into the hot oil, a few at a time. Continue frying until golden brown. Remove with a slotted spoon; drain on paper towels. Dust with sugar.

Makes 8 servings

Capped Almonds

3 cups flour
2 teaspoons baking powder
¾ cup sugar
2 tablespoons dark rum
3 eggs
¼ teaspoon salt
¾ cup butter *or* margarine at room temperature
½ cup whole, blanched almonds
Vegetable oil
Sugar

Sift flour and baking powder into a large bowl. Stir in sugar and rum. Add eggs, 1 at a time, beating well after each addition. Blend in salt and butter. Combine all ingredients using a wooden spoon or the dough hook of an electric mixer. If using mixer, begin on low to blend, then adjust mixer to high for 5 minutes. Turn out dough onto a lightly floured board; knead until smooth. Cover in plastic wrap and chill for 30 minutes.

Roll out dough to ¼-inch thickness on lightly floured board. Cut into 1 x 2-inch strips. Place an almond in the center of each strip; shape dough to fit around almond.

Heat oil in skillet with deep sides or use a deep-fat fryer heated to 375°.

Gently slide dough into the hot oil, a few at a time. Fry until golden brown; remove with slotted spoon. Drain on paper towels.

Roll in sugar. Place on wire rack to cool.

Makes approximately 2 dozen

Chocolate Doughnuts

3¾ cups flour
6 tablespoons cocoa
1 teaspoon salt
4 teaspoons baking powder
½ teaspoon ground cinnamon
2 tablespoons butter *or* margarine
1 cup sugar
2 eggs
1 cup milk
1 teaspoon vanilla

Sift together first 5 ingredients. Cream butter; gradually add sugar and continue beating until light and fluffy. Add eggs, 1 at a time, beating well after each addition. Add milk, vanilla, and flour mixture alternately, stirring until blended.

Roll out on lightly floured board to a ½-inch thickness. Cut with floured doughnut cutter; set doughnuts aside, uncovered, for 20 minutes.

Heat oil in a deep skillet with high sides or use a deep-fat fryer heated to 375°.

Slide doughnuts gently into hot oil; fry for 3 to 5 minutes or until brown, turning the doughnuts as they rise to the surface. Drain on paper towels.

Makes approximately 2 dozen

Capped Almonds, this page

Index

Index